Carville-by-the-Sea
San Francisco's Streetcar Suburb

Woody LaBounty

Outside Lands Media

Copyright © 2009 by Stephen W. LaBounty

All Rights Reserved. No part of this book may be reproduced in any form or by any means without written permission from the author, except for the inclusion of brief quotations in a review.

ISBN-10: 0-9823461-0-7
ISBN-13: 978-0-9823461-0-5

Published by: Outside Lands Media
P.O. Box 460936
San Francisco, CA 94146-0936

www.outsidelands-media.com
www.carville-book.com   Printed in China by Global PSD

Acknowledgments

I used to roll my eyes at the enormous thank-you lists leading off some books, imagining them just author conceits to give friends and relatives a small bit of fame. These absent-minded writers always end by apologizing to even more forgotten helpmates.

Now that I've steered an unsteady ship into port with the creation of this book, I am properly chastened by the ridiculous amount of help I received along the way, and know I, too, am forgetting key contributors.

Grant Ute, Emiliano Echeverria, Angus Macfarlane and John Freeman got my facts straight. For sharing indelible images, memories, and, in some cases, the hospitality of their homes, I thank Art Penniman, Jaci Pappas, Greg Gaar, Ken Malucelli, Glenn Koch, Bob Herbert, David Gallagher, Yvonne Cangelosi, Paul Melzer, Gary Stark, Frank Lemus, Gail Trimble, Scott Anderson, Brian Riggs, Paul C. Trimble, Jack Tillmany, and the late Mark Adams.

I have a huge crush on all librarians and it has not diminished in the least with my experience gathering ephemera and photographs from great institutions.

For treading the Carville path before me, saving me hundreds of hours of research, and giving me inspiration from the high quality of their work, my terrific admiration goes out to Natalie Jahraus Cowan, Jennifer Reese, and the late James Heisterkamp.

Rob Keil's generosity with advice and encouragement has blown me away. I was well-educated by Patricia Chytrowski and Dave Stevenson. Lorri Ungaretti and Richard Brandi gave many hours of their time editing, for which I am very grateful. Artist Lauren Redniss' terrific biography, *Century Girl*, acted as my inspiration. Check it out.

To my dear wife Nancy, I must say: the long hours of labor you put into bringing home bacon have not been misspent, despite my vegetarianism.

To my daughter, Miranda: I understand you will feel disillusioned when you discover that Daddy's job as an author means he pastes old photos into a book and makes people pay to look at them, but note I did write a few captions. And remember that time at the playground when I pushed you on the swing?

I would be remiss not to thank my old friend Stubby for nothing, and will happily be very remiss in that regard.

Additional facts, figures, and sources on Carville can be found at www.carville-book.com

Thanks to you too, Mom!

Introduction

Television programs formed my childhood tastes and aspirations. (I was born in Santa Rosa, California, in 1965, and raised in San Francisco's Richmond District.)

My favorite game show was *Treasure Hunt*. The set held gift-wrapped boxes of all sizes and colors, some on risers, some on the ground. The contestants' not-so-onerous task was to choose a box. Success didn't require esoteric knowledge, hand-eye coordination, or humiliation, just good luck and a willingness to be surprised. Every box contained *something*. It was like Christmas every week, and in my mind, much better than guessing the sticker price of a catamaran on *The Price is Right*.

My friends and I also lived for *The Wild Wild West*, which featured grown men living the dreams of ten-year-old boys: spy cowboys with rappelling lines hidden in their boot heels and false beards tucked in their valises. Their judo moves defeated megalomaniacal villains with doomsday Gatling guns. The best part? James T. West and Artemus Gordon lived in a private train car with secret rooms and compartments for weapons, code-breaking machines, and communication devices.

To me, Carville, a community of old cable and horse cars turned into homes, is *The Wild Wild West*, where a moving vehicle from the 19th century is repurposed and sublimated. Since the car houses melted into the fabric of a commonplace neighborhood, Carville is also *Treasure Hunt*, with the prizes wrapped in stucco and shingles and deceptive additions.

When I pull on my end of the wishbone on Thanksgiving I picture myself in a Carville home at the beach. Since I can't afford to buy even the humblest home in San Francisco, writing this book is likely my best way of getting there.

"t is not the privilege of everyone to own a street car home."
—Flora Haines Loughead
  The Traveler, December 1898

The author and relatives living in a Richmond District garage on Lake Street.

The "Heymanville" section of Carville about 1899, looking northwest from roughly 47th Avenue and Kirkham Street.

A City of Cars*

Suburbs were invented in the 1800s. Before then, Americans were, as the children's fable goes, country mice or city mice. Suburban mice, with three-car garages full of lawn-care products, did not yet exist.

Suburbs mean commuters, and commuting in the era before automobiles required cheap and reliable public transportation. Rail fares around large cities had became affordable for the average businessman by the 1840s, and lines of steam trains and horse cars—rail cars pulled by horses—began spidering out from city cores, allowing the creation of the first "street car suburbs."

The owners of the Park & Ocean Railroad didn't actually have commuting suburbanites in mind when they built a steam train line to San Francisco's Ocean Beach in 1883. Rather, they sought the nickel fares of recreation-seekers, families escaping their apartments and flats for Sunday picnics, entertainment at seaside roadhouses, and the roar of the Pacific Ocean.

In the era of the six-day work week it was a welcome escape to board the "P&O" at Haight and Stanyan streets for a two-mile ride to the beach. Passengers on the right side of the train had a vista of Golden Gate Park, a thousand acres of man-made verdure and scrub, while those on the opposite side beheld to the south miles of rolling sand dunes, nicknamed the "Sahara of San Francisco."

A rustic station shed at 49th Avenue (now La Playa Street) and "H" Street (now Lincoln Way) marked the first beach stop, and starting in the mid-1890s, a few unusual homes settled into the sandy hillocks across from this station.

Architectural historians might describe these strange beach cottages as vernacular structures, created with available resources to address local needs. But these first domiciles were also *vehicular*, a street car suburb literally made of street cars.

Old horse cars and cable cars, retired from service as public transportation, became beachside clubhouses, restaurants, summer homes, bohemian hangouts, residences for poor schoolteachers, and assignation points.

Magazines and newspapers as far away as London and Paris admired the fashionable quirkiness of its residents and the inventive construction techniques that could employ as many as ten old horse cars in one "mansion."

*Throughout this book the use of the term "car" refers to vehicles of public transportation rather than automobiles. Think street cars, horse cars, cable cars...

This community, called *Cartown*, *Carville*, or the more poetic *Carville-by-the-Sea*, welcomed writers and artists who drank into the night, singing revolutionary songs to the surf. Inventors, real estate speculators, criminals, lady bicyclists, politicians, newspaper editors, and capitalists all inhaled ocean breezes from old boarding-platform verandas. Horse cars that once hauled commuters now hosted formal dinner parties.

Concrete sidewalks eventually replaced plank paths on the dunes, water mains pushed out windmills, and conventional homes began to outnumber the car houses.

Refugees from the 1906 San Francisco Earthquake and Fire moved in, and the odd "city of cars" melted into a conventional residential neighborhood. Soon, only the most intrepid could discover the rare cable car hidden beneath a façade of shingle or plaster.

Carville wasn't unique. As older forms of transportation gave way to more efficient methods across the nation, similar car communities arose in Washington State, Massachusetts, New York, Connecticut, and elsewhere. But San Francisco, always a center of eccentricity, innovation, and glorification of the offbeat, took the idea to its height.

The great street car settlement of Carville was located in sand dunes south of Golden Gate Park and near the Park and Ocean train line (shown in red).

A Brief History of Transit

For the story of Carville to be fully appreciated, some knowledge of public transportation in the 19th century is required, since the creation of the car settlement depended upon the obsolescence of different forms of transit. Horse cars ceded route lines to cable cars, which succumbed to new electric street cars. Outmoded, surplus cars became Carville's "building stock."

Mass transit began with animals. Before the Industrial Revolution, animals were the engines of civilization. Humans pulled the carts, oxen dragged the plows, and horses carried or towed people from place to place. No one could travel faster on land than on the back of a horse. When steam engines arrived in the 1830s (their force measured in "horsepower"), local transit systems continued to employ engines of real horseflesh. The ruling form of urban public transportation in the 19th century was the omnibus, a large coach pulled by a team of horses.

The first omnibuses appeared in San Francisco in 1851, carrying up to 18 passengers from Portsmouth Square to Mission Dolores for 50 cents apiece, $1.00 on Sunday. Competing omnibus lines soon covered the city.

By the 1860s horse-drawn omnibuses traveled all over San Francisco, even as far as the Cliff House overlooking the Pacific Ocean.

Horse Car Heaven?

Steam trains gave someone the idea of using locomotive-style rails for omnibus lines. Rails made muddy roads passable where an omnibus might get bogged down, and the reduced friction eased the horses' work. These improvements allowed for larger cars and quicker route times. Coaches pulled on rails by horses became known as "horse cars."

New York City and New Orleans had the first horse cars in the 1830s. After the establishment of a very successful line connecting Boston and Cambridge in 1856, the combination of horse and rail spread widely. Soon Chicago, Baltimore, and San Francisco all had horse car lines.[1]

The early financial successes of horse car lines said a lot about the changing demands of city work. Since horse cars went only a little faster than walking—about four to six miles an hour depending on grades, loads, and traffic—people had to be tired and pressed for time to use them. The coaches were notoriously crowded, and while the fares were cheap, walking was cheaper. Only a fourteen-hour day of factory work could make a horse car ride home inviting.

Horse car lines generally turned a profit, but they also offered a litany of headaches for the companies that ran them. Horses were expensive, costing anywhere from $125 to $200. Feeding the beasts represented about a third of business operating costs. Horses could be temperamental and skittish in crowded city streets, and an epidemic could wipe out most of a company's stock. In 1891 alone, the Eighth Avenue Railway in New York City lost 1,116 horses to disease.

And then there was the waste. Walking city streets in the 1860s meant being confronted by the persistent smell and sight of horse urine and feces. Each horse dropped over ten pounds of fecal matter onto the street daily and hundreds of horses a day could pass a downtown block.[2]

Many believed the problems attendant to the use of horses—epidemics, food expenses, animal waste on the street—could be solved by machine.

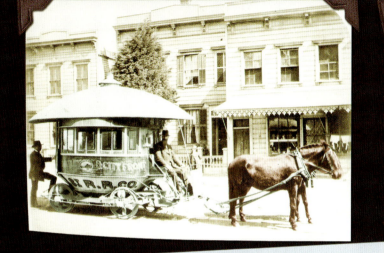
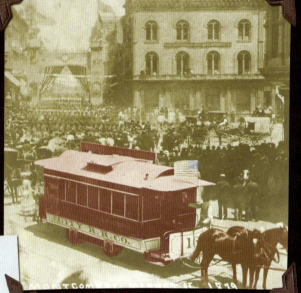
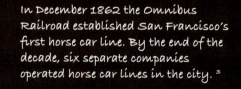

In December 1862 the Omnibus Railroad established San Francisco's first horse car line. By the end of the decade, six separate companies operated horse car lines in the city. [3]

End of the Animal

One obvious solution to the woes of horse car lines seemed to be steam engines, which cost less to run and provided more horsepower than horses.

Unfortunately, steam power had serious compatibility issues with cities. While cheaper once in operation, the initial cost for a steam engine was far higher than a bunch of horses, and heavier weight often meant laying whole new rail lines. The noisy engines, filling the air with clouds of smoke and steam, often scared horses and created dangerous runaway situations. In an attempt to fool the horses, companies tried covering steam engines with wooden horse car-like bodies, creating "steam dummies." Horses were not deceived by the disguise.

Some municipalities banned steam power on city streets, and steam usually supplanted horse cars only on long-distance, semi-suburban lines.

In San Francisco, both horses and steam engines were useless on the steeper hills where the grades and poor traction defeated both animals and engines.

On August 2, 1873, Andrew Smith Hallidie demonstrated a new solution: the cable car. From a powerhouse a steam-driven engine pulled a braided steel cable on a loop just under street level. Traveling on rails, each cable car had a mechanism—a *grip*—that clamped onto the moving cable to start, and released it to stop (with the help of a brake). The first cable car line opened on Clay Street on September 1, 1873, but the efficiency of the system became evident when a second cable line replaced a former horse car route on Sutter Street. The line attracted almost a million more yearly passengers while its operating costs fell thirty percent.[4] Cable technology made the steep hills of the city available for development, and San Francisco expanded to the Western Addition and out through the Mission District on cable car lines.

Adapting to cable cars did mean facing huge initial costs to tear up the streets for the elaborate apparatus. Other issues, such as crossing lines, with cables having to run under cables, became logistically difficult. Backing up wasn't easy (release the cable and push the car), and there was no variable speed. Other than coasting on declines, the cars were stuck going a constant nine miles an hour.

Cable cars had their heyday. Chicago had the world's largest cable car system, with 82 miles of trackage, and at one time San Francisco had eight separate cable car companies in operation.[5] Five cable lines ran on Market Street alone in the 1880s.[6]

Some horse car lines succumbed to steam lines, and some of both gave way to cable lines. As each replaced the other, inconsistencies in gauge and technology meant a surplus of obsolete cars. This problem only increased with yet another new type of car: one run by electricity.

San Francisco had more than 20 cable car lines in 1891. By the 1950s only three remained.

The United States' first steam-powered city railway started in San Francisco on July 4, 1860. (Above, on Market Street.) In 1867, it was replaced by a horse car line. [7]

"It is safe to say that the days of the cable are numbered, save, indeed, on such hills as California and Washington streets, for the trolley system has an infinity of advantages, not the least of which is its flexibility." [8]
—The Wave, March 12, 1898.

The Shock of the New

Electric street cars scared people at first. They could run twice as fast as a cable car, which made them more dangerous to pedestrians. The first cars were also unreliable, but by the late 1880s the kinks of electric trolley technology had been worked out and the benefits were clear.

Electric cars ran cleaner than horse and steam lines, and could go just about anywhere cable cars could go for less money, less infrastructure, and at faster speeds. An electric line required one-seventh the initial investment of a cable line, and once in operation only cost half as much to run.[9] Electric power could accommodate larger cars and the trolleys used the power more efficiently than cable cars. If a cable car company wanted to run just one car the whole system had to start up at the powerhouse to get the cable moving. An electric trolley car drained from wires only what the one car required.

Heavy investment in the other systems kept electricity from immediately taking over. Electric cars also required overhead wires to operate, and public dislike of such visual clutter delayed trolley lines from New York to London. San Francisco banned overhead wires on major thoroughfares, and only the haste to rebuild quickly after the 1906 earthquake and fires allowed electric cars to take over on Market and Geary streets.[10]

Because of their high speeds, electric street cars were initially thought too dangerous. By the 1910s, however, the wire-charged cars were San Francisco's primary form of public transportation.

Above: Market Street in 1917. Right: a cartoon from the San Francisco Examiner in 1896.

ACT 1

The origins of Carville's building stock are explained

Reuse and Recycle—Creating Carville's Building Stock

In 1895, E.P. Vining, the general manager of San Francisco's Market Street Railway Company, had a problem. Actually, he had many. Since accepting his position the year before, Vining's job consisted of one difficulty after another.

Vining's company had formed in 1893 when the Southern Pacific successfully devoured a number of competitors and gained control of two-thirds of San Francisco's trackage. The men who ran the Southern Pacific were among the most ruthless capitalists of the 19th century, and could be difficult bosses. They had made the Market Street Railway big and powerful, but to Vining that just meant his problems were also big and powerful.

From the day of his appointment as general manager, Vining faced immediate and persistent labor issues; squashing emergent union activity became almost a full-time job in itself.[1]

City newspapers and national periodicals relentlessly attacked the company for its monopolistic practices and corrupt entanglements with the government. The Southern Pacific and its Market Street Railway were nicknamed "The Octopus," because of tentacles reaching into multiple industries, strangling fair competition

and squeezing the average worker's wallet.

Out of jealousy, competition, or a higher sense of fair play, some rich and powerful also railed against the company. Adolph Sutro, a very wealthy public figure, had just been elected mayor of San Francisco by running on a progressive platform made up of one plank: the Octopus must go.

On top of all of this, the elephantine Market Street Railway Company was undercapitalized. Expenses had to be cut. Revenues had to be increased. Most of the cars ran on obsolete technology, pulled by noisy steam engines, awkward cable lines, or real horse power. In addition to being slower than modern electric street cars, all these antiquated cars cost more to operate. Changing over would be costly, and also meant a political battle. The public didn't like the unsightly overhead wires that electric power required, and a law banned such wires on the city's main artery, Market Street. But electric cars were the future, and the Market Street Railway would move to electricity wherever possible.

And there was Vining's problem for the day: what to do with all the old cars? Some could be recycled. The cable cars sucked up from the former Omnibus Railway would be switched to electric cars. Unfortunately, most of the horse cars and many of the old cable cars just couldn't be adapted and would just have to make way for progress.[2]

And soon. The company's car barn at Utah and 25th streets had more space dedicated to obsolete stock than to active money-making cars. Another barn at Turk and Fillmore streets, full of old horse cars, needed to be demolished for a new electric car facility.

No other transit company would be interested in cars pulled by an animal. Demolishing the cars or hiring some company to haul them off just represented more wasted capital.

Yes, Vining had many problems. For this one, he decided upon a little experiment. He took out an ad in the papers.

"The Octopus,"
San Francisco Chronicle
February 17, 1895

Liquidation

In early 1895, the Market Street Railway Company placed ads in newspapers as far away as Sacramento offering old horse cars for $20 with seats intact, $10 without. Vining could save the money of disposing of the old cars, and squeeze a bit more cash from them on their way out the door.

Who would want to buy them? What possible use could someone have for an obsolete horse car? The company offered some suggestions in the ad:

> Can be used for newsstands, fruitstands, lunchstands, offices, summer-house, children's playhouses, poultry-houses, toolhouses, coalsheds, woodsheds, conservatories, polling booths, etc.

It is a credit to the imagination of the Market Street Railway that the old cars were employed for most of these suggested uses. Creative souls from all social strata found use for the old horse cars.

The poor inhabited them both as temporary and permanent residences. A line of "decrepit cars" in the North Beach neighborhood served as shelter for the destitute. A rancher near the city's biggest cemetery housed his large family in one old horse car.[3]

The middle class used cars for business. Milton Lee, a "thrifty cobbler," turned a yellow and white Montgomery Street car into his new shoemaker's shop on the corner of Sacramento Street and Central Avenue. A watchmaker did business on the south side of Pacific

Sacramento Record-Union ad, February 12, 1895.

FOR SALE.

THE MARKET-STREET RAILWAY COMPANY, San Francisco, offers for sale a number of condemned

CAR BODIES.

PRICE WITHOUT SEATS, $10 EACH OR WITH SEATS - - - $20 EACH

Can be used for newsstands, fruitstands, lunchstands, offices, summer-houses, children's playhouses, poultry-houses, toolhouses, coalsheds, woodsheds, conservatories, polling booths, etc. Apply to H. O. ROGERS, Division Superintendent, corner Fourth and Louisa streets, San Francisco. MWF

Street near Hyde Street in an old bobtail car, while a dyeing and clothes cleaner moved into a car on a Mission Street lot.[4]

The wealthy used cars as eccentric summer cabins, even as houseboats. James McNeill ferried four old Market street cars across the bay to Belvedere and nailed them together on a raft, creating a two-unit houseboat for his extended family. He painted the scow snowy-white, named it *Nautilus*, and soon the "carboat" was joined by similar craft such as the *Alameda* and *Belvedere*. This odd floating colony, nicknamed "Arktown," lasted until at least 1903.[5]

Another car purchaser, C.A. Hooper, took up the Market Street Railway's playhouse suggestion. He bought an old Mission Street car for the backyard of his Bernal Heights home, and surprised his daughter Ida with it as a birthday present. The car still had its original paint announcing its former destination of "Woodward's Gardens," an early amusement park that stood at 14th and Mission streets. Hooper replaced the wheels with wooden supports, and installed a new floor, a stove, and wainscoting. With some lace curtains in the window, Ida Hooper had a unique playhouse.[6]

Houseboats, stationary floating craft, first made their appearance in San Francisco Bay in the 1890s, brought over as an idea from similar boats on the Thames River in London. By 1900 the calm waters near Tiburon were crowded with the fashionable "arks."

Cars in the Dunes

Charles Stahl was one of the first to show the potential of the old cars as residences. While some husbands bring work home, Stahl, a gripman for the Ellis Street line, turned his work into his home. For $45, he bought three North Beach & Mission line horse cars and paid an additional $27 for delivery to a lot he purchased on the west side of town. The real estate map defined the new home site as on 20th Avenue between J and K Streets,* but "avenues" and "streets" were still optimistic projections at the time. Stahl moved his wife and children onto a windy knoll in a vast desert of rolling sand dunes.

The land cost just $500 and required only a small deposit to secure. The down payment, cars, transportation, and materials all cost less than $100.

Stahl created the car house by himself in his spare time before moving in. He used a stilted wooden platform to keep the three cars above the shifting sands, with their short ends facing the Pacific Ocean to the west and Mount Sutro on the east. He added a covered breezeway at one side to create a hallway through which one could enter each car as a separate room. The northernmost car acted as the kitchen and dining room, the middle as bedroom shared by the whole family, and the last car served as sitting room and storage area. The family moved into their unique abode in the summer of 1895.[8]

THE HOUSE MADE OF STREET CARS.
[Sketched by an "Examiner" artist.]

"The wind blows very strong out in that neighborhood, and the people in the vicinity expect some night that Mr. Stahl will be blown entirely away, each car taking a different direction."[7]

— San Francisco Examiner
September 22, 1895

*Today's Judah and Kirkham Streets.

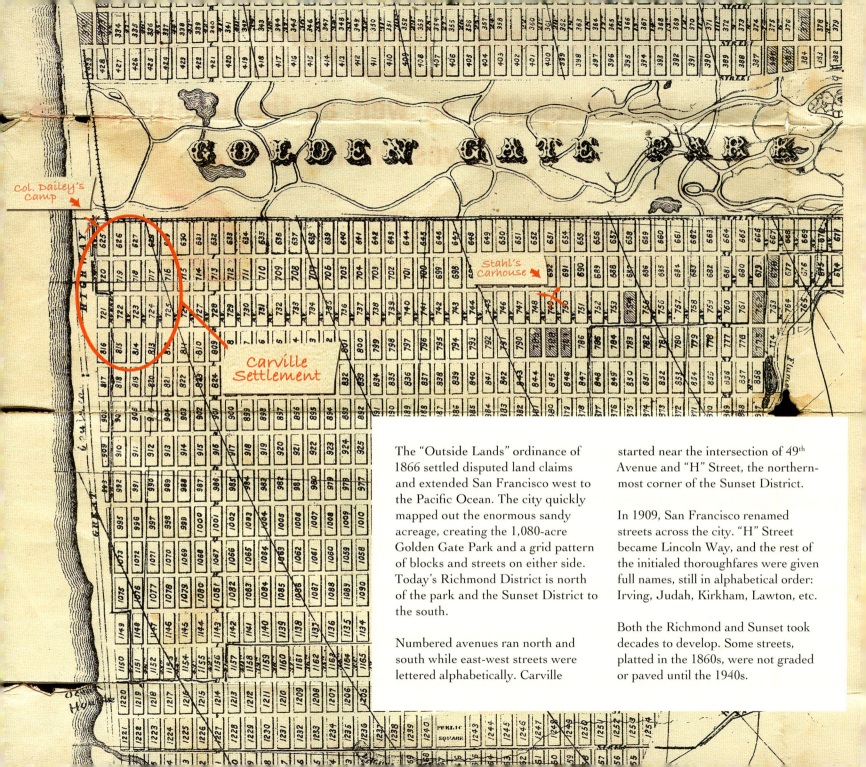

The "Outside Lands" ordinance of 1866 settled disputed land claims and extended San Francisco west to the Pacific Ocean. The city quickly mapped out the enormous sandy acreage, creating the 1,080-acre Golden Gate Park and a grid pattern of blocks and streets on either side. Today's Richmond District is north of the park and the Sunset District to the south.

Numbered avenues ran north and south while east-west streets were lettered alphabetically. Carville started near the intersection of 49th Avenue and "H" Street, the northernmost corner of the Sunset District.

In 1909, San Francisco renamed streets across the city. "H" Street became Lincoln Way, and the rest of the initialed thoroughfares were given full names, still in alphabetical order: Irving, Judah, Kirkham, Lawton, etc.

Both the Richmond and Sunset took decades to develop. Some streets, platted in the 1860s, were not graded or paved until the 1940s.

Selling Sand

E.P. Vining's experiment was a success. Between 1895 and 1901, the Market Street Railway replaced all but one horse car line. Over 200 vehicles, a third of the stock, were liquidated.[9]

Of the many people who took up the company's offer of old horse cars, two in particular set in motion San Francisco's great street car settlement of Carville.

A real estate agent named Jacob Heyman bought one of the Market Street Railway's North Beach & Mission line horse cars for use as a sales office in the Noe Valley neighborhood. There he sold lots from a large subdivision he had immodestly named the "Heyman Tract." At the same time, he was trying to unload sandy properties near the beach, even farther west into the wilderness than Charles Stahl had settled with his triple-horse-car house.[10]

Selling real estate in the future Sunset District wasn't easy. The *San Francisco Call* described the area as a "veritable desert" and explorers were cautioned "to be careful to select a fine, clear day, as it is possible for one to get lost and wander about for hours should a fog come up."[11]

To increase interest in these beach lots, Heyman announced in September 1895 that he had built a "pioneer residence" south of Golden Gate Park: a two-story, eight-room house for Mr. William Gercke. The house stood on 48th Avenue, or *would* stand on 48th Avenue as soon as someone graded streets through the sand dunes.[12]

Despite Heyman's talk of pioneer status, Gercke's home wasn't the first man-made structure in the area. If the constant ocean breezes blew just the right way, Mr. Gercke could spit out his bedroom window and hit the encampment of Colonel Charles Dailey.

Dailey had moved to the area two years earlier, appropriating an abandoned realtor's shed on city block 624—an unmarked section of sand owned by millionaire Adolph Sutro. The Colonel claimed he had Sutro's permission to move into the shack, which had no plumbing, gas mains, or insulation, but did have a window. By 1895, Dailey had built a substantial compound around the shed, including the addition of some horse cars.

In September 1895, the same month Jacob Heyman announced building the beach's pioneer home, the *San Francisco Examiner* made reference to Dailey's camp:

> Two old Valencia-street cars have been lying in the sand at the end of the car line at the Beach for some time. Some one bought them for a speculation. Mayor Sutro re-bought them for a bigger speculation. Now they are to be opened as a coffee saloon…[13]

The coffee saloon Dailey opened in an old horse car would be the seed of a legendary community, and Jacob Heyman, the ambitious real estate man, would soon be inspired to help that seed flower in the beach sand.

Where Some of the Old Cars Have Gone to.

Sutro's Sand Dunes

Adolph Sutro, owner of block 624 and mayor of San Francisco, thought big. Scheming on a grand scale is what made the Prussian immigrant a millionaire.

In the 1870s, he dreamed of an enormous drainage tunnel for the rich Comstock silver mines in Nevada. The potential of it, the sheer audaciousness, drew in the investors. Sutro got the project built and got out at the right time, cashing in his stock and retreating to San Francisco a very wealthy man.

In the 1880s, he thought big when he rebuilt a slightly disreputable roadhouse on the northwestern tip of the San Francisco peninsula. Sutro's new Cliff House rose over the ocean as a seven-story Bavarian castle, a wedding cake made for gods.

In the 1890s, Sutro built an enormous public natatorium, or bathhouse, beside the Cliff House. Sutro Baths, powered by the waves of the Pacific Ocean, featured seven pools of differing temperatures and Sutro surrounded the pools with every wonder that ancient culture, sideshow hucksterism, and taxidermy could buy. Both water slides and real Egyptian mummies were under one roof.

Sutro established his personal estate on a promontory overlooking both of these monumental projects. The grounds were a pleasure garden of exotic topiary, flower beds, foreign trees, ferns, gazebos, Greek statues, and ornaments. Unlike his millionaire peers, who reclused themselves in great gated estates down the peninsula, Sutro invited in the public, making his home a pleasure park.

When Sutro began collecting books he didn't stop until he ended up with 250,000 volumes and one of the world's great libraries.

He started tree-planting projects on his enormous land holdings—at one time he owned a twelfth of San Francisco—until he had covered the city's central hills with a vast forest.

When many thought the west side of town, named the "Great Sand Bank" on some maps, was uninhabitable, Sutro imagined the city growing into these "Outside Lands." He predicted the plots of sand would be worth ten times what he paid for them and envisioned "solid rows of housing" filling the dunes by 1902.[14]

In 1894, Sutro thought big again and, defying the political machines of the time, ran successfully for mayor of San Francisco on a progressive platform.

So why did this man of big dreams dump some old horse cars onto his sand dunes? Did he see them as odd curios, not too different from the stuffed jaguars he bought to decorate the concourse of Sutro Baths? Or did he, as some speculated, use the cars in a scheme of "improving" the land to get a better tax rate from the city?[15]

While planning ocean-fronting mansions on his dunes, the promise of a little rental income, even from worn-out horse car shells may have been enough to entice Sutro's penny-pinching and pragmatic side. The Sunday crowds disembarking from the Park & Ocean rail stop had nickels in their pockets to spend on refreshments, and renting the cars out might start some kind of community on the empty land.

As the new mayor of San Francisco, Sutro had more than enough to occupy his mind. He expected that, eventually, the wealthy would pay to build grand estates on his beach lots; in the meantime the cars more than paid for themselves.

Plus, Sutro even had a caretaker already on site in the form of Colonel Charles Dailey.

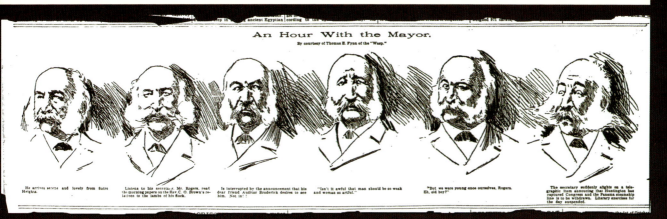

San Francisco Examiner, January 19, 1896

"Mr. Sutro, who had the imagination to build the biggest and ugliest baths in America, and a Cliff House that looks like a fortified dry goods box, has but to close his eyes and see a vision of pale pink palaces embowered in verdure along the boulevard stretching over the sand dunes to the gum trees in the distance, and all paying tribute to his foresight." [16]
— The Wave, September 11, 1897

The Old Man of the Sea

The first resident of Carville never actually lived in a horse car. Colonel Charles Dailey claimed to be a Civil War veteran, a former government agent in Arizona, and just an aging man in poor health who counted himself a friend of Adolph Sutro. Whether the Colonel was ever in the military is unclear. As newspaper columnist Millie Robbins wrote in 1963, "every other gentleman of the last century was called either *colonel* or *captain*, and frequently for reasons totally unrelated to formal rank."[17]

Adolph Sutro received many letters and visits from strangers asking for jobs, favors, business starts, and outright charity. Dailey's relationship with the rich man may have originated in this manner. Whether an old friend or tolerated squatter, Dailey moved into a beachside real estate shed on Sutro's land around 1893.

Miles of dunes isolated Dailey from any neighbor or store. The land, identified by the city assessor as *Outside Lands Block 624*, had no plumbing, gas, sewage, or paving. The weather, especially in summer, tended to cold, windy, and foggy. Into this remote outpost, ostensibly on Sutro's advice, Colonel Charles Dailey settled "for his health."

Sutro may indeed have prescribed beachside living to Dailey, as sea air was popularly thought to be salubrious. The millionaire lived at the ocean's edge himself, and declared that the beaches had "no smoke, no sewer gas, no decaying matter—nothing to injure the health."[18]

Colonel Dailey's Camp

Somehow the Colonel convinced his wife, L.M. Dailey, to join him. She cooked their meals over a campfire in the dunes until the Colonel procured an oil stove and expanded the shed with driftwood to make a kitchen.

The Daileys mostly relied on the waves to provide supplies. Every morning the Colonel walked the beach, combing for souvenirs and useful items. He strung wire through washed-up coconut shells for a fence. To keep shifting sands from blocking his front door in the night, he paved a path with gathered sea shells. The wreck of the *City of New York* in October 1893 gave Dailey lumber to build shelves and stairs to a sleeping loft. While the Daileys had some chairs and a couch, a visitor wrote that the "remainder of the furnishings consist primarily of things washed up from the ocean."[19]

The Daileys decorated the cabin with bottles of every shape and hue, starfish, bits of coral, bird wings, rusty swords and guns, hats, a pair of opera glasses—all amid "numberless sleepy, stretching cats." Dailey invested his informal museum of scavenged curiosities with stories of faraway lands: this sponge came from the West Indies, this broken drum from the South Sea Islands, this silk slipper from China, and this bit of snow shoe from an Inuit's foot in Alaska.[20]

Despite the jumble, an 1897 photo of the home reveals a clean, comfortable room. Mrs. Dailey sits doing needlepoint at her sewing table. The Colonel reclines in a rocker with a book, his great coat and scholar's fez on.

In the "garden" around their home the Daileys set out lanterns, flapping flags, and bird cages—one holding a particularly noisy green parrot. The Colonel took to calling his camp *Beachside*, and painted the word in bold white letters on the roof of the house. Cora Older, a friend of the couple, admitted that while the name conjured up visions of a Newport estate, "to those not under the spell of the beauty of the ocean 'Beachside' is not an attractive spot, for shrubbery does not grow readily there, and back of one lies a stretch of sand hills."[21]

The area felt a great deal less isolated on Sundays, when thousands of pleasure-seekers disembarked from the Park & Ocean train for a day at the beach. Recent grading and paving of the boulevard along the beach made the corner even more heavily traveled with walkers, bicyclists, and horse-drawn cabs. Dailey's growing encampment started gaining notice from the public, and Dailey noticed back. Perhaps, with Mayor Sutro's permission, a little money could be made from these weekend hoards.

Park & Ocean Railroad

On December 1, 1883, the opening day of the Park & Ocean Railroad, more than 10,000 riders took the trip from Haight and Stanyan streets to the Ocean Beach. Passengers rode in open cars pulled by steam dummies and steam locomotives on H Street (now Lincoln Way) beside Golden Gate Park. The shifting dunes that drifted over the rails, sometimes even between hourly trips, often forced employees to stop the train and shovel sand.

This steam line opened up the beach to the great masses of the city and introduced many people to the western half of San Francisco, which, while mapped as part of the city since 1868, was generally considered a wilderness.

Previously, getting across the dunes meant a long walk over the sand or using a toll road for 50 cents. Now whole families could go for a day of picnicking and wading in the surf quickly and relatively cheaply. A horse-drawn omnibus held 15 passengers maximum, but one trip on the P&O could take 360.

The Market Street Railway, and by proxy the Southern Pacific, owned the Park & Ocean Railroad. The company at first charged a five-cent fare without transfers, which meant unless riders lived within walking distance of the station at Haight and Stanyan streets, most had to pay five cents just to get to the P&O, or ten cents total to get to the beach.

This no-transfer rule infuriated Adolph Sutro, who had a monetary interest in cheap fares west to his pleasure resorts and the land he hoped to sell in the area. Idealistically, he was also rankled by the monopolistic power of the Southern Pacific. Sutro's populist battle against the company led him to build his own steam line along scenic Land's End and eventually found him sitting as mayor of San Francisco.

The Market Street Railway did eventually bow to the pressure and allow valid transfers to connect to the beach, again making a ride to the beach a nickel for everyone. On March 18, 1898, the line converted to electric trolleys.[22]

Park and Ocean steam dummy.

Park Beach & Cliff House Railway.

"...the brisk, bracing, healthful, pure salt sea air is well worth the long ride to the beach and back. It is better than medicine."[23]

—San Francisco Call, 1896

The First Four Cars

In 1894 or 1895, Dailey took on four abandoned horse cars from Sutro, rented at $5 a month, and opened one as "the Annex," a coffee saloon and refreshment stand. After adding a few picnic tables and umbrellas, Dailey hosted open-air luncheons and dinners. He posted his bill of fare on a wave-worn plank nailed to a post: "Sandwiches, Doughnuts, Fruit, Lemonade, Root-Beer, Chewing-Gum, Cigarettes, and Other Refreshments."[24]

Judge George P. Gough rented one of the other three cars as a getaway on Sundays and holidays. A bachelor, Gough ensured his privacy by painting some of the windows and hanging lace curtains in the others. Inside, he sectioned his car into two rooms. One he designated as a sitting room decorated with Japanese art, small rugs, and cushions. The other half of the car, furnished with a hair mattress, acted as the judge's bedroom.

The Falcons, a ladies bicycle club, moved into a car just a short distance from Gough. In the 1890s, bicycling was a raging fad across the United States, and the nation wrung its collective hands over the sport's particular popularity with the female gender. Bicycling liberated women from the confines of home and, in search of sensible riding attire, some women shocked society by wearing blousy-trousered "bloomers" instead of skirts or dresses.

In 1894, *The Traveler* magazine noted that "for weeks the columns of the *New York World* have teemed with letters from the dear public about the propriety, impropriety, sanity, insanity, healthfulness and unhealthfulness of bicycling for women."[25] In the same issue, a columnist published a letter to the magazine that railed against bicycles, asserting no lady "would ride one of the horrid things." The columnist disagreed, calling exercise "healthful and invigorating" and bicycling "very fashionable."[26]

Fashion and society were definitely part of the Falcons' interest in the horse car clubhouse. Mrs. Fitzgerald, the club's ringleader, rented the car not only as a place to rest after rides—the long, upholstered seats served very well for naps—but as an interesting locale for the seven married ladies to entertain. Sunday morning rides to the beach were followed by breakfasts and card games in the car, and soon the women hosted dinner parties as well.

The Falcons were as attentive to decoration as Judge Gough had been. The Falcons' car sported alternating curtains of blue and white denim in the windows, matching blue and white coverlets upholstering the long seats, and blue and white matting on the floor. Between the windows, the ladies hung paintings of bicycles and seascapes At the back of the car, the Falcons added a kitchen and shed for their bicycles. Three coal oil stoves fueled dinners for as many as 35, although parties that large took place *al fresco*.

The Falcons mounted the car on a wooden raft foundation to keep it from sinking in the sand, and surrounded it with a low wire fence. A short swing gate allowed entry beneath an arch featuring the club logo. On the roof of the car, the ladies mounted a bicycle wheel.[27]

The last of the first four cars in Carville, a dark red Valencia Street line car, was rented by Mr. and Mrs. Fitzgerald and Mr. and Mrs. White as a private car where they "might retire to rest, smoke, and gaze on uninterrupted ocean."[28]

The Lady Falcons and admirers in front of their clubhouse.

The Falcons (as remembered in 1913):
Mrs. Ida Fitzgerald, President.
Mrs. William Leonard, Secretary.
Mrs. Viola Rice, Treasurer.
Mrs. Dr. Edson, Vice-President.
Mrs. William Miller, Mrs. F. Lisinski, Mrs. Gillman, and Mesdames Cox, Le Long, Rice, Orpin, and Sutton.[29]

"For weeks the columns of the New York World have teemed with letters from the dear public about the propriety, impropriety, sanity, insanity, healthfulness and unhealthfulness of bicycling for women."

—The Traveler, 1894

A Thriving Suburb

In July 1896, the *San Francisco Bulletin* published an article about the Daileys, their street car-inhabiting neighbors, and the rustic charms of living at the beach. That October, the *San Francisco Chronicle* called the community a "thriving little suburb." In May 1897, the *San Francisco Call* finally took a look at the "little colony." Dailey told to all the visiting media a well-practiced tale of being near death until the restorative powers of the sea air saved him.

In September 1897, the colony was referred to as "Carville" for the first time in print. *The Wave*, a periodical edited by the soon-to-be famous novelist Frank Norris, also featured the first published photos of Carville. An interior shot of one car revealed that even in a small space a Victorian's love for sumptuous ornamentation could prevail. Tapestries, floral throws, and filigree of all kinds covered the space from top to bottom. The author noted that the cars could only be rented, not owned, since Adolph Sutro had grander plans for the land.

By late 1898, the colony had seven cars in addition to Dailey's encampment. The Falcons were now joined by a matching group of male bicyclists. These "wheelmen" modified an old Mission car to the point of invisibility, erecting an outer shell to create an extra room with large windows, and divided the structure into three sleeping rooms, a kitchen, and a large closet.[30]

"Den decoration runs riot in the houses."

Converting Rubbish into Beauty

In contrast to the nonconformist Colonel Dailey, those moving into Carville were Superior Court clerks, judges, insurance brokers, and newspaper editors. All had the means to own, and did own, conventional homes. Why were they retreating to old street cars? One writer explained the appeal as the "spice of adventure in appropriating something that is cast away," and in turn "converting to a thing of beauty what is ranked as worthless rubbish."[31]

Whether for health, escapism, or the challenge of transforming trash into beauty, those who planned to move to Carville needed to prepare. *The Wave* warned that "shops do not deliver goods so far from the city limits," because Carville was not "a center of population."[32]

That would shortly change.

Cora Older wrote one of the first articles on the future Carville in 1896, calling it "Beachside." Left: Early car houses on the northwest corner of Block 625 (today's Lincoln Way and La Playa Street) in 1897.

Colonel Dailey visits a neighbor in the late 1890s, his white "Beachside" cottage and Annex coffee saloon visible in the distance.

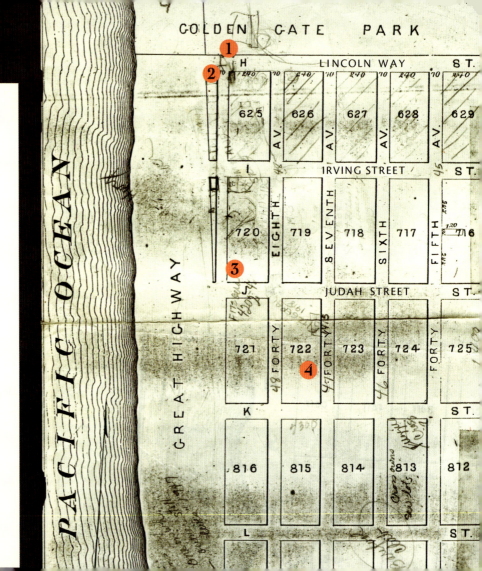

Beachside Blocks and Carville's Birth

1 A station stop for the Park and Ocean Railroad — a simple shed — stood on "H" Street (today's' Lincoln Way) at the edge of Golden Gate Park. The line veered north at this point, terminating near the Cliff House.

2 Colonel Dailey lived at the northwest tip of block 624, a narrow strip on city maps. Adolph Sutro owned both 624 and block 625, where the first car houses were created.

3 Jacob Heyman's beachside sales office, water tank, and his first car houses.

4 Location of "Heymanville," a neighborhood of Carville created in 1899, south of the Sutro-section.

Living-room and dining-room in two-car house

A house near 44th Avenue and Clement Street built around a car, with another in the backyard in 1907.

Act 2

Heymanville and how to build a Car House

Novel Cottages

In 1895, Jacob Heyman had proudly announced building the pioneer residence at the beach. Four years later, still the only "real home" in the area, the house was surrounded by old horse car clubhouses.

Heyman must have been frustrated. It wasn't that the real estate broker didn't appreciate the reuse of old vehicles—he himself had bought an old horse car for his office in Noe Valley—but there didn't seem to be any real money to be made off of them. In fact, the presence of old horse cars brought down the appearance of the neighborhood Heyman and others were trying to create, likely lowering what they could charge for a beach lot.

Heyman and other realtors in the area didn't dream at Adolph Sutro's level—chilly Ocean Beach wasn't going to become the French Riviera—but they hoped to attract some middle-class buyers, and the cold, remote dunes were a tough sell. One real estate man remembered, "We would advertise and people would ride out in their buggies. Most of them would scoff at us and tell us to peddle our sand somewhere else."[1]

For all of Sutro's grand ambitions for the land, he bent his dreams enough to allow the first car houses to occupy it. Jacob Heyman had to acknowledge that at the beach repurposed horse cars were more popular than conventional homes. Why should he second-guess the public? Perhaps street cars might sweeten the sand dunes.

In January 1899, Heyman advertised an ocean lot available for monthly installments of $7.50. For an extra $35 up front he would throw in two old horse cars. The ad response was decent enough that Heyman stockpiled more cars from the transit companies. Over a dozen of them had to be trucked out through the recently paved Golden Gate Park roads and dragged across the sand to an entire block Heyman owned at 48th Avenue and Judah Street.[2] There, listing in the sand like ships in a swell, the cars awaited owners to claim them. By February 1899, Heyman had ten families living in his new community. He not only rented and sold cars without modification, but began building car houses: "seaside novel cottages on easy terms."[3]

"...the village of Carville grew up on the white dunes, looking as though a gigantic box of toys had been spilled and scattered there." [4]
—Overland Monthly, 1908

Heymanville

Heyman didn't use the name "Heymanville," preferring "the Health Resort of San Francisco," "Sunset Beach," or, eventually, "Carville."

Using a car as a sales office, Heyman enlisted one of his first customers, Mrs. Rodgers, as an agent to staff it. Next door to it, the real estate man showed just how novel a seaside cottage could be, erecting a three-story building of cars facing the Pacific Ocean like some mechanistic pre-Columbian temple.

People came to gawk, and many couldn't walk away without renting or buying a car house of their own. A *San Francisco Call* reporter aptly described the appeal of Heyman's business plan:

> [When] one can, without going through the agonies of house-hunting or the miseries of house-building, order a cozy yet commodious "hand-me-down" residence one day and have it delivered on the lot the next, ready for occupancy, one of the problems of civilization seems to have been solved.[5]

As the neighborhood grew, Heyman worked on infrastructure to support his colony. George Robinson, one of the first buyers, remembered that when Heyman sank his first well everybody laughed, figuring any water hit 500 feet from the Pacific Ocean wouldn't be fresh. Heyman struck gold in an aquifer, providing the area with its first essential service: water. He dug more wells and erected windmills and water towers.[6]

In July of 1899 a reporter estimated over seventy street car homes in Carville, and added to the name the ironic suffix of "by-the-sea," in imitation of tony seaside resort towns of the time. "Carville-by-the-sea" soon had neighborhoods within the neighborhood. The section of original Sutro-owned cars next to the park and rail line were called "Cartown." Here, either because the cars were rented or owing to the pioneers' simple tastes, modifications were few. Car houses looked more like cars than houses.

South of Cartown stood "Heymanville," where private ownership prevailed and so the population naturally succumbed to the allure of home improvement. Residents modified and expanded their car houses until "cottages, villas, Swiss chalets, castles and towers began to rise in every direction."[7]

By 1900, the advertised price for a lot and two cars was up to $600, and reports of the novel community appeared in newspapers as far away as New York and Washington, D.C.[8]

Heyman office on right

An antler-decorated car for rent

Sand baths would often be thrust upon Carville residents. Nightly winds shifted dunes so that in the morning one side of a car might be submerged, while the other end had a three-foot drop to the ground.

To prevent their homes from sliding and shifting, some residents drove wood pilings deep into the dunes as foundations.

Residents of heymanville

George Robinson may have been Heyman's first car house customer. He paid $650 for his land and cars, including delivery, to build "Dad's Home" in January 1899. Robinson embraced the whimsicality of his home, decorating its exterior with deer antlers.

Mrs. S.D. Rodgers, a retired schoolteacher, initially bought a beach lot as an investment. When her finances became low, the possibility of car living inspired her to move onto the lot with her daughter. She had two cars placed end-to-end and raised up to create a ground-floor level. A colleague, **Mrs. A.K. Staples,** followed suit by stacking two cars atop two others to keep the ocean's waves in sight.

Dr. Charles Cross built one of the first private car clubhouses, using as a nucleus two double-ender cars that formerly ran on the Woodward's Gardens route in the Mission District. Cross believed "sand baths" improved health, and tried to take credit as the community's pioneer resident in support of his theories. The doctor would be responsible for introducing many San Francisco artists and writers to the charms of the beachside community.

Robert and **Ida Fitzgerald** had rented one of the first Sutro-owned cars for the Falcon Bicycling Club, then another as a weekend getaway. By 1899, they had totally given in to their desires to live full-time at the beach. They purchased a lot on the corner of 47th Avenue and Judah Street, where they raised two horse cars to a second story. They would spend the rest of their lives in their car house, which still stands today.

Down the street from the Fitzgeralds stood one of Carville's grandest and most elegant structures. At 1338 47th Avenue, **Mrs. Patriarch** ran the two-story "Vista del Mar" as a 1890s version of a bed-and-breakfast inn.

She left two former North Beach and Mission cars visible on the upper floor of her establishment so potential guests knew the Carville "mansion" truly was a car house. With a windmill and water tank attached to the back, the entire structure formed an elegant U, its breeze-protected courtyard home to masses of flowers. The former boarding platforms of the car were capped in graceful bentwood curves at the corners of the second level. Extensions to the building on the north side created a rambling maze of car rooms with connecting hallways.

Among a fashionable set that wanted to experience a bohemian weekend getaway, but for whom a drafty car on the dunes was just *too* much to handle, the Vista del Mar became a popular destination.

Vista del Mar,
1338 47th Avenue

"We encouraged any kind of building at first—even the old horse and cable car houses that made up Carville—just to get someone out here."[9]
—Jules Getz, realtor

The Andrus Home

Roy Andrus bought property on 48th Avenue just south of Lawton Street in the early 1900s and fenced in on his lot a few small cottages, including one made of two cable cars. Various family members came to visit, including Roy's brother-in-law, Fernando Cortez Ruggles, who was an enthusiastic photographer.

Using his 1903 *Century* camera, Ruggles captured some of the best scenes of Carville life. One of Ruggles' daughters, Mabel, became a postcard collector, and sent her father's prints around the world in trade, signing her address as "Carville." One correspondent became her husband.

Unfortunately, many of Ruggles' glass plate negatives were lost when his widow used them to create a backyard greenhouse. Roy Andrus moved to Palo Alto in 1913, but his car house lasted at least into the 1920s. Descendant Jaci Pappas still owns Ruggles' camera.

1608 48th Avenue

Photos of Ruggles family members at 1608 48th Avenue and a more conventional home at 1350 48th Avenue. Jaci Pappas posing with her great-grandfather's camera.

Building Methods

Creating a car house required some planning; while some homes consisted of a single car, many were made of multiple cars. One car house creator apparently incorporated *ten* cars in one structure. Floor plan compositions sound like an alphabet soup as weekend architects made L's, U's, X's, I's, T's and more.[10]

New car house construction about 1900.

"Some h'ist 'em up and build a house underneath, some put two alongside and rip out the walls, some put 'em end to end, some make chambers of 'em and some settin'-rooms. They call the colony Carville-by-the-Sea, and it looks for all the world like some new-fangled sort of Chinatown."[11]

— "The Picaroons,"
Gelett Burgess and
Will Irwin, 1904

"The platforms of the cars are often transformed into balconies and bay windows with the aid of the carpenter and glass fitter..."[12]
— Scientific-American, 1901

George W. McCallum's home, built in the Heymanville section, facing the Great Highway about 1899. McCallum worked for San Francisco's Recreation and Park Department.

The Vista del Mar in its later incarnation as St. Andrew's Episcopal Church. The building stood on the east side of 48th Avenue, between Irving and Judah streets, until at least the mid-1920s.

The U-Plan

The "U" arrangement set either three cars at right angles, or connected two cars with by a non-vehicular section.

Mrs. Patriarch's *Vista del Mar* elevated the cars to a second level, but the blueprint could be used with a single-story structure as well. The great benefit of this alignment was a courtyard shielded from wind and billowing sand, elevating body temperature on cold foggy days and protecting gardens from being engulfed by dunes.

The courtyard also gave a semblance of privacy, which was difficult to achieve in buildings with walls of windows.

A postcard view of Vista del Mar, circa 1901.

"Three cars set in the form of three sides of a square give a good opportunity for an open court—a hammock, flowers, a bench or two, serve to make such a court enticing." [13]
—Four Track News
January 1906

The I-plan

Two cars connected end-to-end by a wood or even canvas shell made up the I-plan. Usually one car served as the public space, or living room, while the other car acted as a den or bedroom.

Vestibules between cars could involve wholesale removal of walls or just a covering to keep the wind and sand out. The connecting section itself might be a closet, bathroom, kitchen, or a combination of any or all. Often structures were elevated off the ground by posts to create a basement for the easy installation of bathtubs and later, running water. At least one Carville owner installed a sunken tub accessed by trapdoor. When not in use, the tub and door were camouflaged by a rug.[14]

Doubling the I-plan created the "Maltese Cross," a configuration of four cars with ends meeting at a center building. Multiple vacationing families or guests could have their own wing and garden area, while meeting for meals and conversation in the middle room.

A Heymanville cottage near 47th Avenue and Judah Street about 1900.

The Maltese Cross

"...in a car kitchen the shelf that held the [horse car] lamp makes an excellent spice cupboard." [15]
—Outing Magazine
January 1903

Kitchen in single-car house

The L-Plan

Perhaps the most popular configuration in multi-car houses was the "L." Dozens of examples were rented out as weekend retreats across the dunes.

The houses were usually arranged with the entry door facing east in the elbow of the structure, which created small yards sheltered from ocean winds.

Facing the Great Highway between Irving and Judah streets, this multiple-car house was one of the more famous, and was featured on postcards such as the one on page 2. (Other views: pages 92 and 94.)

As with many car houses, this structure continued to be added upon and renovated over time until the cars almost disappeared from public view.

Before Carville

Some of the first car houses in the Sutro-owned blocks, such as the Falcons and Fitzgerald/White cars, had long histories as public transportation before becoming beachside abodes and clubhouses.

Built in 1866, the cars were especially large—the biggest horse cars ever to run on San Francisco streets. For three years they traveled Market and Valencia streets, shuttling passengers to and from Woodward's Garden, an early amusement park on 14th Street. Despite the relatively flat route, two horses were required to pull the behemoths, and new, lighter cars replaced them in 1870.

In the 1870s, the cars made appearances on Market Street for rush hour work, but were mostly assigned to the Potrero & Bay View line and 5th Street line.

From 1880 to 1888, four of the cars found new lives as steam dummy trailers on a line connecting the intersection of Market and Valencia streets with Eureka Valley (today's Castro District).

The unwieldy size of the cars—likely 8 to 9 feet wide and 20-24 feet long—made them difficult as working horse cars, but suited their last use as clubhouses.[16]

One of the big cars pulled in the 1880s by steam dummy (a steam engine disguised as a horse car).

Car Comfort

For interior decorating, a few modifications were necessary for long-term and comfortable habitation, but the cars provided a surprisingly elegant starting point. Instead of the plastic seats, Plexiglas windows, and fluorescent lights of modern public transit, a street car from the 19th century presented an atmosphere of almost luxurious craftsmanship, as one writer noted:

> [T]he most ordinary vehicle of this description is an exquisite specimen of cabinet work, finished in choice and highly polished woods, with plate-glass windows, and benches fashioned for both elegance and comfort…[17]

The platforms could be enclosed as closets or sun rooms, although Carville homes didn't really need sun rooms, with every wall lined with numerous windows. A house constructed of three or more cars might have up to 30 windows letting in light. In the often-foggy climes, the sun had "to take the place of furnace and steam pipes." At night, all those windows didn't make for well-insulated rooms, so a good oil stove was required.[18]

Curtains regulated temperature and ensured some privacy. Many residents choose alternating colors, say blue and white. The high ventilator windows allowed in ocean breezes, but kept out most blowing sand. Many residents painted marine scenes on these small windows.[19]

Passenger seats were lengthened for beds, or taken outside for garden benches. Boarding platform signs were used as fencing around these beach gardens, which usually featured nasturtiums and pelargoniums.[20]

A number of writers noted that the San Francisco climate, with a limited rainy season and winters free from snow and ice, went a long way to making a year-round car house a practical possibility.

While some people brought in lumber and professional carpenters, many followed Colonel Dailey's example and created their additions from whatever the sea happened to wash up.

When the ship *Reporter* went aground on Ocean Beach in 1902, Carvillians began scavenging. The *San Francisco Call* predicted that over the following two weeks the "picturesque little burg by the sea will have the greatest building boom in its history."[21]

Mary Gunn

Pioneer Anxiety

The glee of creating this new neighborhood was tempered in the Sutro-owned section. Adolph Sutro died in his cliff top cottage in 1898, and quickly there were claims upon his estate by relatives, civic institutions, charities and business partners. Sutro's generous nature during his life gave almost anyone who knew him hope that a little of his fortune might be available for the taking. As his estate went into probate, Sutro renters waited anxiously, knowing whoever ended up owning the beachside blocks would have more ambitious plans for the property than street car homes.

Mrs. Mary Gunn was one of these Sutro renters, holding a prime car to the south of Dailey and the Falcons, facing the Great Highway. Mrs. Gunn used her car as a tea room and restaurant where "notable bohemians dined." Mrs. Gunn could be a bit erratic with customers, serving only those whom she took a liking to, expelling those not meeting her standards. *San Francisco Bulletin* editor Fremont Older and his wife Cora rented a car next door and were frequent customers and unofficial guardian angels to the irascible restaurateur, covering her rent when she fell behind in payments.[22]

While scores of new neighbors, business competitors, and new odd structures surrounded him, Colonel Dailey was closing in on a full decade of dune living. In January 1902, a *San Francisco Call* reporter came out for a visit.

Dailey told his tales once again, how he gave his all to his country in various positions and aided the wounded on the fields of

Gettysburg, how he counted Adolph Sutro and railway magnate C.P. Huntington as friends.

Once profiled as a carefree bohemian, now Dailey appeared a much lonelier man. His benefactor Sutro and other claimed famous acquaintances were dead. His wife had left him and was "living in the East." After years of service to his country, he now lived forgotten "among skeletons" in a house made of driftwood. With Sutro gone, and the blocks around him growing in popularity and value, Dailey understandably feared being evicted, and told the reporter "If I could only be sure of my little place I would be so happy."[23]

A block south, where people *could* be sure of their place, buying lots and cars from Jacob Heyman, Carville was a hit. By 1902, one hundred cars were in use at the beach, and a few new "real homes" were even being built amid the car houses.[24]

Families, even wealthy ones, came to rent cars for the summer. Bars and restaurants like Mrs. Gunn's opened in humble cars with pretentious names such as "Villa Miramar" and "Chateau Navarre." Stories on the offbeat community were published in New York and London, and some of the most accomplished writers and artists in San Francisco were drawn to visit Carville-by-the-Sea.[25]

CARVILLE POSSESSES A VERY POPULAR RESTAURANT, AND SOME OF THE NOTABLE BOHEMIANS OF THE CITY MAKE IT A PRACTICE TO DINE HERE

Mary Gunn's about 1908

"The extinct horse-car reappearing in the form of a fixed dwelling is a favorite resort of the Californian, who has not read for nothing the various home magazines with their inspiring hints on how to make a summer cottage out of a pair of rubber boots."[26]

— Juliet Wilbor Tompkins, 1903

Colonel Dailey profile in the San Francisco Call, January 5, 1902

Act 3

Haunt of Bohemia

A Haunt of Bohemia

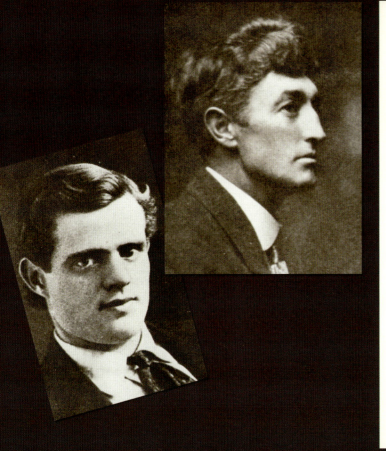

At Carville, writers, artists, and philosophers seeking inspiration, insight, or just privacy made cars into poets' garrets and painting studios. The globe's mightiest ocean crashed endlessly against a great continent right outside. Beach living fulfilled the artistic stereotype of existing at the margins, without the trappings of society or material comfort, just the mind for companionship and contemplation as sustenance.

It was also a good place to have a party.

Dr. Charles Cross, of the sand-baths-for-health plan, offered his car as a clubhouse to a group of writers, philosophers, and painters. The artists came for inspiration, to inhale the seas breezes, and to lighten the doctor's larder. Cross made it easier for them by keeping an open account at a nearby grocer.

Carville had its share of dilettantes and poseurs, but the circle Cross attracted consisted of some of the most accomplished artists in San Francisco.[1]

Car houses near 48th Avenue and Lincoln Way.

"The car companies are glad to dispose of them at a small price and they have furnished many a charming cottage to artists and others of the take-life-easy-tribe..."[2]
—Sarah Comstock
1906

Les Jeunes Fix Coppa's

Giuseppe Coppa's humble Italian restaurant, which occupied a shabby corner of the Montgomery Block building downtown, needed a bit of sprucing up. Most of his customers were artists and writers, generally impoverished, who frequented Coppa's because of its proximity to their cheap rented studio space upstairs and for its prices: a mere quarter bought spaghetti, bread, and a pint of wine.

To elevate the atmosphere, and perhaps draw in patrons willing to pay a bit more, Coppa painted the interior walls a cheery bright red.

Then Porter Garnett took over. Garnett was a fine printer and calligrapher, one of a group of regulars that arrived after hours to meet at one of Coppa's large round tables to talk art, philosophy, and politics.

Sometimes the group went by the name *Les Jeunes*, ("the Young"), but wags dubbed them the "Fuzzy Bunch," in reference both to the scruffiness of their grooming and the opaqueness of their ideas and nonsensical outbursts.

Taking turns both reveling and reviling at the table were editor Mary Edith Griswold; novelist and essayist Jack London; humorist Gelett Burgess; painter Xavier Martinez; poet George Sterling; artist Maynard Dixon; and other writers, philosophers, and free-thinkers such as Will Irwin, Ina Coolbrith, and Anna Strunsky.

Rarely in agreement about anything, the artists came together in their displeasure over the new color scheme. Garnett led the way in persuading Giuseppe to let them repaint Coppa's with some artistic flair. Over an extended weekend, the Coppa Murals were born.

Within a border of stenciled black cats created by Martinez, the walls overflowed with caricature, graffiti, cartoons, quotes, and irreverent prose. Depictions of Griswold and writer Isabel Fraser welcomed diners in fairly realistic glory, but the other regulars appeared in caricature, swimming in a fog of devils, nymphs, and injunctions of Latin, Italian, and French.

The outrageous murals did the job. Coppa's soon became crowded with tourists goggling at the visions while bending ears for bon mots from the artists' table.[3]

As much as the Fuzzy Bunch enjoyed attention, the crowds at Coppa's made a quiet horse car clubhouse at the beach an attractive occasional getaway.

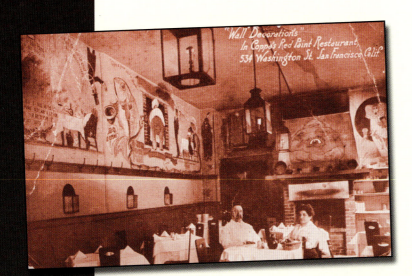

Anna Strunsky

Anna Strunsky, patronizingly named the "girl socialist of San Francisco," used her experiences as a Russian-Jew and her Stanford education to debate with anyone. She had a close friendship with Jack London, and the two of them added gravitas to many social gatherings with their fiery discussions on Socialism.

Strunsky later married a man of wealth, and with her capital, was able to continue the fight for the underclass in Washington, D.C.[4]

Mary Edith Griswold

"Maisie" Griswold wrote one of the best-known articles on the 1906 San Francisco earthquake and fire, recounting the confusion, despair, optimism and the oddly mundane moments as she wandered around by herself seeking friends and shelter.

A frequent visitor to Carville and a muse to artists for her charm and editorial skill, Griswold had many admirers. Proposed to by telegram by Edwin Emerson in the chaos after the earthquake, she married him in Robert Louis Stevenson's house later that year.

On one visit to the Cross car house in 1914 she sent to her husband, who was on assignment in Mexico, a "Greetings from Carville" telegraph signed by Vail Bakewell, Maynard Dixon, Dr. Charles Cross, and Xavier Martinez. In it, the artists wished their best to revolutionary general Pancho Villa.[5]

Photograph by Arnold Genthe.
Mrs. Mary Edith Emerson.

Edwin Emerson

As the husband of Mary Edith Griswold, Emerson was a loose associate to the Fuzzy Bunch. He visited Dr. Cross's car house a number of times, and accompanied the artists on a bicycle ride commemorating the Falcons' tenth anniversary in 1905.

A war correspondent, one of Teddy Roosevelt's Rough Riders, and an Olympic medal winner, Edwin Emerson was also a great storyteller and name-dropper. His grandson Art Penniman remembered that telling tales was essentially Emerson's occupation in later years.

In response to a reminiscing newspaper column in 1950, Emerson wrote a long letter to the *San Francisco Chronicle* enumerating every member of the Fuzzy Bunch and their beachside high jinks.[6]

Gelett Burgess

Probably the artist who found the most inspiration in Carville was writer and humorist Gelett Burgess. With his coauthor Will Irwin, the puckish Burgess featured the neighborhood of street car homes in two novels.

Just five feet, four inches, Burgess made up for his lack of physical stature with a bigger-than-life personality, "bellowing like a bull," singing cowboy and French revolutionary songs, and wearing outfits that ranged from bright yellow overcoats (his neighbors nicknamed him "the walking peanut") to what one writer called "strange skins and crimson robes."[7]

Despite lifelong ambitions to be known as a serious writer, Burgess's fame came from his humorous pieces. He invented *The Goops*, circle-headed miscreants of negative behavior, who had among their fans the children of Theodore Roosevelt. As the editor of a quirky literary journal, *The Lark*, Burgess penned a nonsensical quatrain that haunted him the rest of his life.

Gelett Burgess.

So sick of having his doggerel repeated back to him wherever he went, Burgess invented a comeback.

I never saw a Purple Cow,
I never hope to see one,
But I can tell you anyhow,
I'd rather see than be one.

Ah, yes, I wrote the Purple Cow—,
I'm sorry, now, I wrote it;
But I can tell you Anyhow,
I'll Kill you if you Quote it!

 Goops

City Railroad cars between 47th and 48th avenues, Irving and Judah streets (wheelbarrow imagined).

The Tale of the Retired Car-Conductor

In *The Picaroons*, one of Burgess and Irwin's heroes gets tossed into jail after being caught in a raid at a Chinatown lottery. In the cell is Eli Cook, a "regular customer" whom the police say is always arrested for begging, but is found to have plenty of money on him. When this odd vagrant worries aloud that someone might steal his street car while he's in jail, the new cell mate laughs and asks, "How can a street car be stolen?" Cook tells his story.

As a conductor, Eli Cook made a fortune pinching nickels from the fare box. By ingenious methods he beat all fare box designs and loss-control systems to steal about $12,000 of the company's money. The crooked conductor retired and bought a lot at the beach. When old cars were offered for sale, he purchased the very one he used to work aboard, number 27, for ten dollars:

> I hired a dray and moved the thing out to the Beach that very afternoon. I set it up on two sills on my lot, calculatin' I could use it for a cabin to hang out in, over Sunday, and it was as steady as Plymouth Rock, and made as cute a little room as you'd want to see. Every time I went I tinkered round and fixed her up more, till I had a good bunk at one end, lockers under the seats, and a trig little cellar beneath, where I kept canned stuff.

> 'Twa'n't long before I regularly moved out there and stayed for good. Just from force of habit, I expect, at first, I rung two bells every time I got on, and one bell before I got off, and I always keep it up, just as if the old car was really on the rails. I never went in and set down but I felt as if No. 27 was poundin' along toward Woodward's Gardens, with the hosses on a jog trot. Sometimes when the rain was drivin' down and the wind blowin' like all possessed, and it was pitch dark outside, with the surf rollin', I'd put down my pipe and go out on the platform, and set the brake up just as tight as I could. I don't know why, but it kind of give me a sense of security.

The old car started coming alive to the conductor, rattling and shifting in the sands. Doors stick, lights go out, and Cook realized the car was remonstrating him for his life of graft. To mollify number 27, he had to drop a nickel in the old fare box every time he entered, and turn in the proceeds when the box filled up.

Even after Cook paid back the company in full, the car kept shivering and settling. It wasn't until the former conductor joined another car to his as a mate that the ghostly movements ceased. Soon after, the unusual couple produced a red wheelbarrow.[8]

Assignations

Gelett Burgess's novel *The Heart Line* (1907) revealed not only a detailed description of a Carville house, but also one of the less-publicized uses for a lonely car far from town. The heroine in the story, Fancy Gray, is taken on a date to the beach by Mr. Gay P. Summer, where the gentleman had a car house "of the more modest breed." Burgess gives a detailed description of the car and its utility:

> It was a weather-worn, blistered, orange-colored affair that had once done service on Mission street. The cash-box was still affixed to the interior, the platform, shaky as it was, still held; the gong above, though cracked, still rang. There was a partition dividing what they called their living-room, where the seats did service for bunks, from the kitchen where they were bridged for a table and perforated for cupboards. There was a shaky canvas arrangement over the plank platform; and beneath, in the sand, was buried a treasure of beer bottles, iron knives, forks and spoons and wooden plates.
>
> Here, unchaperoned and unmolested, save by the wind and sun, Gay P. Summer and Fancy Gray proceeded to get acquainted. They made short work of it.[9]

The "Water-Wild" car clubhouse on Great Highway between Lincoln Way and Irving Street, circa 1906.

Great Highway, between Irving and Judah streets, 1905.

Martinez in His Studio.

(Not in Carville.)

Xavier Martinez

Mexican-born painter Xavier Martinez — called "Marty" by his friends — was an accomplished artist, founder of the California Society of Artists, and longtime teacher at the California Academy of Arts and Crafts in Oakland.

Martinez wore corduroys and a crimson tie every day, and his wild hair made one writer speculate that there must be "some bitter feud between Martinez and the tonsorial profession."[10]

He was also remembered as very jealous of his young and pretty wife, Elsie Whitaker. When one guest showed her a bit too much attention at a party, Martinez went in the backyard, drew a quick caricature of the man, pinned it to a tree and began taking pistol shots at it.[11]

Black cat stenciled border by Martinez for Coppa's restaurant.

BURIED BENEATH SHIFTING SANDS

Efforts to Sink a Well at the Ocean Beach Almost Terminate in a Shocking Tragedy

A strange incident that nearly terminated in a tragedy happened on the bleak sand dunes south of the Cliff House during Sunday's storm. Manuel Nicholas, a Greek, was digging a well and the sides caved in on him. The hole was some ten feet deep and the shifting sands made it a difficult task for the rescuers, who, however, fought death inch by inch and finally presented the Greek to his sobbing wife in a condition that might be described as "slightly disfigured, but still in the ring."

The rescuers were a band of merrymakers—artists and writers—who now laughingly tell how they "jollied" Manuel and kept his wife at bay, for at times she came dangerously near the edge and another "cave in" was momentarily expected. It happened in this way:

Xavier Martinez, the well known artist, has taken up his abode in the remotest car of Carville, with the intention of doing some sketching far from the madding crowd. But, despite his

isolated situation, Martinez finds that strenuous times follow him. Sunday he invited a number of his friends to dine with him, promising them a Mexican dinner cooked by himself. A Slav named George W. Weldon came over the sand dunes to the hungry artists and asked them to help him dig a well. "We came not here to dig wells," answered Martinez. "We are here to rest and eat and listen to the story of the sea." Whereupon the Slav hailed Manuel Nicholas, who, with his wife, was returning from an outing. The good natured Manuel fell an easy victim to the wiles of the Slav, and, armed with pick and shovel, these two foreigners set to work to dig a well in the uncertain sands.

The little crowd in the car dismissed the matter from their minds until they were about to sit down to dinner, when Weldon rushed in with the news that his newly acquired assistant was buried in the well. By this time it was pouring. The men of the crowd rushed hatless across the sand. They found the man buried to his neck and the sand still trickling in. His arms were pinioned, and one of the men in his excitement jumped in, carrying an avalanche with him, that completely covered the unfortunate man.

Meanwhile the sand was pressing on the buried man's chest in such a way that he could not breathe, and he lapsed into unconsciousness. Clarence Wilson, an able-bodied man, shoveled unceasingly. Herman Scheffauer, the poet, stood on a rudely constructed scaffolding hauling up buckets of sand. He was dressed in a cutaway, with a carnation in his buttonhole and a book of Stirling's poems sticking out of his pocket. Charles Unger acted as nurse, running for smelling salts, which he and Malcolm Fraser in turns presented to Manuel when his head was once again in view. Martinez also stood on the scaffolding and held the ends of the rope that was around Nicholas' body, and when finally the weight of sand was removed from his trunk the entire company took hands at the rope and pulled. It was a "tug of war" in real earnest, and the best of every man's muscle was on that rope. When Manuel emerged from his temporary grave a shout went up.

The ladies of the party had meanwhile taken the hysterical Mrs. Nicholas to the car. It was hard to tell which was in the worse condition, Manuel or his wife.

Now Mrs. Nicholas declares that Manuel will never dig a well again.

Xavier Martinez has to save the day in Carville, San Francisco Call, February 23, 1904.

"Light Summer Reading, Served without the Slightest Effort"

In 1910, Waldemar Young mocked the melodramatic fluff publishers offered as "summer reading to tired businessmen" with his own romance set in Carville.

Chapter I

Gwendolyn Overton descended the broad marble steps of her Carville mansion, the lilt of a song on her lips.

Ellis Powell, from the downtown district, was swinging in a hammock behind a hummock. He recognized the sweet air floating on the sweet air. It was one of his favorites, popular at the time: "I Love My Wife, but Oh, You Kid!" The music thrilled him.

Lurking in a deep shadow was Randolph Dearborn, a guilder from Chicago. He was a regular villain, as evidenced by his mustache.

Gwendolyn went back into the house. When she went back, she returned. Nothing happened, but we have all our characters introduced, and that's enough for one chapter.

Chapter II

Once more Gwendolyn Overton emerged from the mansion which her father had built with the profits of his remunerative profession—that of decoying clams from their sandy beds.

This is Chapter II, and it's time to start something.

Gwendolyn was attired in a bathing suit. She was going in for her morning dip. She came out in Chapter I just to be introduced, but now the action of the story starts.

Lightly she tripped down the sands, humming her favorite melody. Ellis Powell had changed his position and was now hanging on the golden gate. It had fond memories for him of childhood days.

As Gwendolyn, unconscious of any danger, tried one toe and then another in the water, Randolph Dearborn, a curse on his lips, sprang from his hiding place and would have seized her, but Ellis Powell let go of the gate and they locked in a death struggle.

Night came on and the sea sighed. At last one man arose victorious.

It was Ellis Powell.

Chapter III

But where was Gwendolyn? You see, we go right along with the story now. We don't wait for anything. She had run like a hunted deer (or dear) down the sands. As she did so she stumbled over a bottle. Looking at it curiously, Gwendolyn discovered inside a letter. Feverishly knocking the top off the bottle, she read:

"Dear Ethel: Meet me at Dibble's." [A beachside roadhouse that stood on the corner of Taraval Street and the Great Highway.]

There was no signature, but the handwriting was Ellis Powell's.

Chapter IV

Fearful that danger lurked near, Gwendolyn quickly sought shelter. The place was warm and a young man stood beside a piano and sang a song. It was her favorite melody.

She had changed her bathing suit for an evening gown.

Suddenly she gave a start, which was inexpensive, and saw sitting in a corner Ellis Powell with a strange woman.

"Where did you leave Randolph Dearborn?" Gwendolyn asked haughtily.

"He's up the boulevard somewhere," answered Ellis, paling.

"I fly to him!" said Gwendolyn. We leave her in midair.

Now, all that ends somewhere, but it's a long summer, and we haven't time just now to finish it. Besides, there is so much to read!

Of course, in the end Ellis Powell and Gwendolyn come to that perfect understanding of each other's souls which goes with the charlotte russe affection of summer between the first chapter and the last. There are adventures and misunderstandings, but the end is as certain as the rising of the sun.

So goes the novel of the day—the book that is written for us in the summer of our discontent. Those deeper, more abstruse problems of life which have their place at other whiles are not served to us these days— unless we hunt in the back rows of the book shelves.[12]

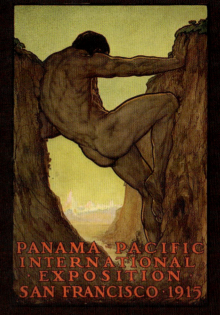

Perham Nahl had dancer Ted Shawn model in the sand dunes at Ocean Beach for his poster, "The 13th Labor of Hercules," used to promote San Francisco's Panama Pacific International Exposition. [13]

Society's Merriest Hours

The birth of Carville coincided with the conclusion of the 19th century, the *fin de siecle*, when artists and the artistically-sympathetic both anticipated and dreaded the end of many things.

The Gilded Age boom times of the 1880s had flipped into an 1890s economic depression. Ostentatious displays of wealth gave way to appearing fashionably carefree, a bit disheveled, even voluntarily impoverished. Society dames invited scruffy, jobless philosophers to tea, and daringly smoked cigarettes in the company of licentious painters. "Bohemian" was the popular adjective of 1896.[14]

With showy extravagance out of fashion and eccentric simplicity in, entertaining in a horse car at the beach, using some wave-worn debris as decorations, could make one a leading light in popular society.

In the spirit of the Falcon Bicycle Club, seven women procured a car they named "A Haunt of Bohemia." Rather than a studio for outcast artists, the car was primarily used for social get-togethers on the weekends. A journalist noted that "[i]nvitations to the dinner parties which are given there are largely sought."[15]

Another club of women rented one of the original Sutro cars facing the Great Highway and rechristened it "Water Wild." The ladies added a porch on the ocean side of the car for card games, and retreated inside for luncheons.

Water Wild reportedly saw the "merriest hours that ever were spent in Carville," although few would consider games of euchre up to the standard of bohemian wildness.[16]

"Bohemian either means too little or else it means too much, and in each case I find it irritating." [17]

THERE is a story told in San Francisco —and who cares whether it be true or not, so long as he likes the story?— that when the old horse-cars were being replaced with gaily painted, brand-new cable-cars, there was a veteran driver who sent in his resignation. The car company offered him a position as gripman, but the old fellow shook his head, thereby waggling a very long white beard, and replied, "You can't teach an old dog a new bark. I don't want to learn how to handle one o' them blame things. All I want's my old car to get old in." So the company gave it to him, and he hauled it out to the beach and made himself an abode.

The "bobtail car," as the much abbreviated horse-car of early days was called, is no longer obtainable, and the new car residences are constructed of well-made cable- and trolley-cars, perfectly sound and in good condition for habitation, even though they are past their best days for track use. The car companies are glad to dispose of them at a small price and they have furnished many a charming cottage to artists and others of the take-life-easy tribe—those who do not care to invest hoarded thousands in a summer home, or haven't the thousands. A very few dollars will fit up a car, and if your neighbor just above is satisfied with nothing less than a ten-room dwelling, each room a separate car, and a windmill whirling high against the sky to mark his abode, what do you care if a portière drawn across your single car marks where dining-room ends and drawing-room begins?

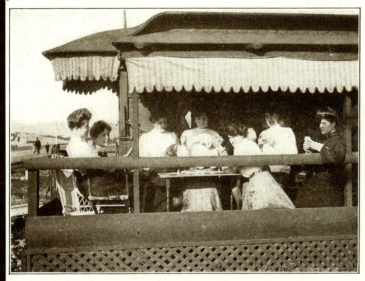

Photo by Bushnell, San Francisco
The euchre club, at "Water Wild"

"Just like other summer resorts, Carville has its Nob Hill and its humble homes on the lower stretch of warm sand. [...] There is a spirit of fraternity, the easy, breezy fraternity of the West, prevailing throughout the little town, and the merry, informal parties given there make those of many a fashionable resort seem dull." [18]

—"Carville"
Four Track News,
January 1906

La Boheme

For a truer debauchery, one could visit *La Boheme*, a car rented by a group of working musicians in the Sutro section of Carville.

Between midnight and seven in the morning, when their various shifts in the city's cafés and music halls came to an end, La Boheme members retreated to the car to drink, and between rounds, take dips in the icy surf.

Henry Newman, the night watchman for *The Louvre* nightclub, attended to the clubhouse by day, stocking the car with food and drink while keeping company with a nameless canary and a dog named Bismark. In addition to the club pantry, the heavier drinkers kept private stashes of alcohol safe in lockers under the car seats. A four-burner coal oil stove served as a kitchen, with utensils "borrowed" from Henry's employer.

Members planted a flagpole stolen from the Tivoli restaurant on "Mount Diablo," a sand hill near the car satirically named after the Bay Area's highest peak.

Because they rented in the Sutro section, the musicians had to keep the outside of their car as they'd received it, with its white number 1 and red paint job intact from its days as a bobtail car for the Market Street Railway.

Inside the car, however, the musicians spruced up the walls with "pictures of all shapes and sizes, posters, verses, bits of doggerel, photographs, clippings from papers, cuttings, beads, shells and a thousand things."[19]

When the Metropolitan grand opera company visited town, the La Boheme car hosted a huge dinner *al fresco*, proving a cohort of heavy-drinking men could throw a dinner party as well as any ladies card club.

Generally, the boys tended to casual goofiness and carousing, and for a newspaper article on the club, the members proudly posed in their swimsuits beside a dead sea lion.

In 1901, Scientific American noted that while many families permanently resided in Carville, the majority used the cars as "opportunities for original methods of entertainment and diversion for themselves and friends." [20]

The La Boheme car, one of the first car clubhouses, stood at the corner of 48th Avenue and Lincoln Way.

Sculptor on the Ocean Beach Makes Artistic Images Out of Wet Sand.

The cold winds of yesterday had a discouraging effect upon the attendance at the Park and Beach, but the few thousand who availed themselves of the clear weather were more than repaid by the spectacle of the great breakers dashing into foam on the beach.

A sculptor with an artistic soul and a facile hand astonished visitors to the beach yesterday afternoon by modeling various figures and portraits in the wet sand on the beach just south of the Cliff House. The largest and most remarkable was a heroic sized figure of a woman lying on her back and clasping a chubby infant to her breast. It was labeled "Cast Up By the Waves." The portraits were those of Longfellow, General Grant, President Taft and other notable men.

The boys and girls who delight in making mud pies or sand pies on the beach were speechless with astonishment and asked the man to show them how to make such nice things.

San Francisco Chronicle, December 6, 1909

The Great Highway, near Irving Street, about 1905.

In 1902, George Cram Cook, an English professor at Stanford University, visited "Street-Car Bohemia," and met "several young artistic couples [...] creating a unique community of impecunity and mirth." Cook remembered someone writing a play about amorous entanglements between two of these couples among the cars. [21]

"With only the boom of the surf for his requiem, the little old hermit with the snowy beard had passed into the great sea of mystery alone..." [22]
—San Francisco Call, 1903

Goodbye to the Colonel

After the turn of the 20th century, many of the professional artists who haunted Carville set up shop in a new seaside retreat down the coast in Carmel (or Carmel-by-the-Sea). Led by George Sterling and writer Mary Austin— who made it a habit to wander around in Grecian robes—a true artists' colony formed among the woods and sands south of Monterey.

Artists, freethinkers, and those who enjoyed keeping company with either, still walked the sandy paths between car houses, but the atmosphere changed, and nothing better signified the exodus of bohemian life from Carville than the loss of its original bohemian.

In 1903, Colonel Dailey passed away in his driftwood cabin. In his obituary, the *San Francisco Call* both noted a transition in the area's character and a new name for the neighborhood by identifying Dailey as the father of what "was once Carville, but is now known as the more dignified title of Oceanside."[23]

ROAR OF WAVES IS HIS REQUIEM

Old Colonel Dailey Slips Into Beyond Alone in His Cabin.

Old Colonel Charles E. Dailey, the father of what was once Carville, but is now known by the more dignified title of Oceanside, is dead. Yesterday his body was found lying in the little bedroom of his driftwood cabin out by the ocean beach, just as death had stricken it. With only the boom of the surf for his requiem, the little old hermit with the snowy beard had passed into the great sea of mystery alone; there was no one to close the dim eyes or fold the wrinkled old hands across the breast.

Ten years ago Colonel Dailey received from his boon companion, Adolph Sutro, a little patch of sand out on the beach below the Cliff House. There he gathered together enough of the flotsam of the set—broken bones of dead ships—to build himself a tiny cabin. The rooftree, clapboards and joists all came out of the sea; not a sliver of wood was there which had not been once a part of some vessel, long since lying broken backed at the bottom of the green depths.

Here, housed in by the skeletons of ships, old Colonel Dailey spent the fading days of his life. For years his light was the only one which winked through the blur of the storms, his little garden spot was the only color in the yellow waste of sands. Then one by one the old street cars began to be wheeled out to the beach and grouped into a mongrel village about "Colonel Dailey's camp." His tiny cabin and flower patch became the nucleus of Oceanside.

The man who had lived so many years with the gulls and the sand pipers had once been prominent in affairs of the nation. A native of Connecticut, he was made military agent of the State when the war of the rebellion flamed out. In that capacity he was on the battlefields of Gettysburg and Fredericksburg in the midst of the fearful carnage. Later, when the war was over, he was appointed receiver of Government funds for the Territory of Arizona and held that position for several years.

But ill health began to wear him down and ten years ago Colonel Dailey forsook the activities of the world to live alone with the roar of the sea and the rush of the salt airs. Alone he was when death came to him on the wings of the mysterious night wind from the west.

DENIZENS OF CARTOWN OUTSIDE THEIR "HOUSE"

A CORNER OF CARTOWN, NEAR SAN FRANCISCO

A "Cartown" Home.

"The Graphic," a British magazine, mixed fact and fantasy in a 1902 article.

"The Boatmen" car clubhouse stood near 47th Avenue and Judah Street.

Cartown

CARTOWN is one of the oldest settlements in the United States. It is near San Francisco, and faces the Bay. All the houses are made of old tram-cars or have these cars introduced in the structure. The first settler in Cartown was a poor Italian, who bought a lot on the beach, and having no means with which to construct a home, conceived the idea of using an old street car as a dwelling-place. There were hundreds of these old horse-cars which had been discarded by the companies with the introduction of electric traction. They were useless to the companies, which gladly sold one of them for 10 dols. The Italian established himself in his old car. The idea caught the popular fancy, and presently there was a demand for old cars from people of moderate means. They were used to establish a summer colony on the Bay. Few of the houses in Cartown are permanent residences, but much ingenuity has been displayed in adapting the old cars to temporary uses. Bath-tubs in some are reached by raising a trap in the floor of the car. Platforms are enclosed and made to serve as pantries, or extended and used as piazzas. One woman has eight cars arranged around a court. Some inhabitants have built second stories above their cars, and some have raised their cars to form a second story above a frame structure. Water from the city is piped to the cars. There is a restaurant in Cartown, and many persons from San Francisco spend their evenings amid its quaint dwellings.

ACT 4

The Rise of Oceanside

"This increased desire to get close to what was once called nature's heart has no doubt an element of fad about it, and as such will die out. Those who take up informal living as they would ping-pong will inevitably throw it down again." [1]

—Outing Magazine, January 1903

House of Silent Light

In 1903, the year of Colonel Dailey's passing, little had changed in the old section of Carville. Adolph Sutro's massive estate, five years after his death, still foundered in probate. With the deceased millionaire now the truest absentee landlord, few improvements came to blocks 624 and 625. Cars still hunkered in ungraded dunes, connected to each other by driftwood planks plopped on the sand.

Outside of the Sutro land, however, sand hillocks started to resemble the grid of the city's official map of the area. In 1903, realtor Sol Getz bought two blocks east of Sutro's land, and began cutting the streets of 46th, 47th and 48th avenues south from Lincoln Way. The year before, Getz had graded the block along the Great Highway between Kirkham and Lawton streets, and sold lots ranging in price from $750 to $2,400. He knew it would take basic infrastructure to get closer to the higher number, and worked on the blocks beside the train line and park first.[3]

Standard amenities of a modern San Francisco neighborhood soon became available to most Carvillians: gas and telephone service, electricity, water lines, local grocery stores, a public school, and a street car to commute to work downtown. With the former limitations of Carville life overcome, more people chose the beachside as a permanent home.

In 1901, Alexander Russell purchased the Oceanside House, an ancient roadhouse at the far south end of the beach, and transformed the remote shingled building into a richly furnished estate. Russell was the type of man Adolph Sutro had always dreamed would settle on his ocean-fronting sand dunes: wealthy, well-traveled, and socially connected.

While Russell had interests in real estate, mining, and the rubber industry, and generally acted the part of a civic-minded businessman, his wife was far from typical. Ida Russell possessed very open-minded and eclectic spiritual beliefs for the times. She studied comparative religion and hosted Sunday morning lectures on Brahmanism, Confucianism, and other Eastern theologies. True believers and the curious came to the former Oceanside House, which Ida liked to call the "House of Silent Light." She explained to one reporter that she studied all religions, taking what she thought best from each.[4]

In 1905, the Russells hosted Zen master Soyen Shaku from Japan for nine months. The entire household, including servants, gave up meat, wine, and smoking, and meditated three times a day. Ida became the first American to begin koan study, and the Russells' invitation and championing of Soyen Shaku gave Zen Buddhism an early foothold in the United States.[5]

"The life has its limitations, but for health and cheapness, the use of a city combined with the delight of a westering ocean, Carville stands unique among seaside colonies."[2]

The old Oceanside House became a private home in 1901, and its owners, the Russells, hosted an eclectic crowd of spiritual seekers and leaders, including Buddhist monk Soyen Shaku. Two Omnibus line horse cars were part of a rear addition to the home.

Oceanside is Born

The Russells created a magnificent Japanese garden around their home, and erected a high wall to protect it from the shifting sands. The imposing fence and the unconventional household—the Russells had adopted a number of children, and hosted a rotating series of guests interested in spiritual enlightenment—soon inspired locals to call the old roadhouse the "House of Mystery." Ida attempted to tone down the gossip, which included rumors of a secret cult.

> There is nothing new or original in what we're trying to do. […] Though we live quietly, we're still vitally interested in the joys and sorrows of the world and our home is always open to neighbors and friends.[6]

To demonstrate his neighborliness, Alexander Russell acted as one of the founders of a local improvement club. On March 7, 1903, he joined realtor Sol Getz and other men with interests in the area to form what they called the "Ocean Boulevard Improvement Club." At the first meeting in Getz's office on the corner of 47th Avenue and Lincoln Way, the group elected as its first president Robert Fitzgerald, the Superior Court clerk whose wife led the Falcons Bicycle Club.

Most of the club members were realtors or owners of businesses in the area. R. Barker sold real estate from 4609 H Street (Lincoln Way) in the nucleus of the original Carville. He owned a lot of land and "was anxious to see the vacant lots sold for home-seekers rather than sold for speculative purposes." (A strange sentiment, since he and his fellow realtors were in the business of land speculation.)

John Brumund, "pioneer grocery dealer of the district" was a member, as was Wallie Jackson, who sold "only the best liquors and cigars" in catering to the "best trade in the district." Carpenter/home-builders such as W.W. Thayer and Peter Leonard—who had built Brumund's new store—were also active members.[7]

Two months later, Getz suggested changing both the name of the group and the community it represented to "Oceanside."

The name was once used for the defunct roadhouse that Russell had turned into his home, and perhaps the members intended a connotation. If a dilapidated public house could be transformed into an estate of wealth, couldn't a bohemian village become a prosperous neighborhood? Getz and Barker wanted to sell lots. Leonard wanted to build houses. Other members wanted infrastructure for flushing toilets and street lights. Perhaps just ditching the name Carville could make these dreams a reality.

Plans were made to turn the tide of public consciousness with large painted signs welcoming people to the newly-named Oceanside.[8]

OCEANSIDE IMPROVEMENT CLUB.

This club was organized March 7, 1903, in the office of Sol Getz Sons, on the corner of Forty-seventh avenue and H street (now Lincoln way).

The names of the first officers were as follows: President, Robert Fitzgerald; secretary, D. Edward Marcus.

The officers for 1909 were as follows: President, W. N. McCarthy; vice-president, A. C. Clark (now deceased); secretary, E. A. Michner (resigned); financial secretary, A. B. Mahoney; treasurer, R. Barker (resigned).

The position of secretary to fill the unexpired term is now held by Joseph McAuliff, and that of treasurer by Peter M. Leonard.

Joseph McAuliff, Secretary

Peter M. Leonard, Treasurer

The untimely death of Vice-President A. C. Clark in October of last year was a sad blow to the club as well as to his friends and relatives. His place will not be filled until the annual election of officers on February 8.

The club has accomplished a great deal for the district, such as inducing the Spring Valley Water Company to extend their mains into the district. The gas and electric light company to do the same was through the efforts of the club. The new school house was obtained almost entirely through the zeal of the members of the club, who worked day and night to secure the building, which was finally completed in 1908. The sewer system was also obtained through the noble efforts of the club, and the contracts for the Forty-eighth avenue sewer are now all ready to be let. The work on the H street sewer

JOHN BRUMUND.

John Brumund, the well known merchant of Oceanside, was born in Germany over 40 years ago, and came to California in 1882 from the city of New York.

He was the pioneer grocery dealer of the district, having a store 11 years ago on Forty-ninth avenue and I street. Two years ago the building was turned into a first-class cafe, and is now operated as such by E. P. Baker and George Hart.

Mr. Brumund has just completed a handsome new store on the corner of Forty-eighth avenue and Irving street, where he has opened up with a large and varied stock of hardware, paints, oils, crockery, glass and household goods of every description.

His son, Frank Brumund, is general manager, and owns a large share of the business. His sister, Ada, is bookkeeper and secretary for the firm.

Mr. Brumund, senior, is a large property owner in the district, and owns several lots and buildings, among them being the Oceanside hall, which he rents for meetings, and which is much sought after by organizations and for parties and balls which are held from time to time in the district.

Mr. Brumund is a member of the Royal Arch and other fraternal societies, and takes a deep interest in the welfare and upbuilding of the district.

He is also an earnest member and worker in the Oceanside Improvement Club, and is a man of pleasing address, and has the faculty of making and holding the friendship and esteem of all with whom he comes in contact.

A WELL-KNOWN REALTY DEALER.

One of the most progressive men in San Francisco today is R. Barker, the Oceanside owner and dealer in real estate, who has an office at 4609 H street, near Forty-eighth avenue. Mr. Barker was raised in the old Bay State of Massachusetts. When the War of the Rebellion broke out, Mr. Barker enlisted in the navy on the Union side and fought with distinction for the flag of his country, and had the proud honor of being one of the number to assist in placing the army flag on Fort Sumpter. He operated with the Army

Sunset Journal, January 28, 1910

Previous Page: Great Highway between Irving and Judah streets, 1901. Right: a closer view of houses on the block.

Improvements?

Whether it was the signs or more personal lobbying, by the end of 1903 the new name started to stick and improvements began. The *San Francisco Call* reported soon after that twenty streetlights were being installed in "Oceanside, formally known as 'Carville.'"[9]

Piped-in water may have appeared in parts of Carville as early as 1901, but most residents still used windmills to pump from wells. On April 7, 1903, the city's Chief Sanitary Inspector reported to the Board of Health that water in five of Carville's nine wells was contaminated by nearby cesspools, and recommended a septic tank. Oceansiders visited the Board of Park Commissioners the next month, requesting that the Spring Valley Water Company be allowed to lay water mains along the Great Highway. The improvement club also petitioned other city agencies for more street grading, a new school building, and a fire station.[10]

The man who turned Carville into a boom town and a viable area for housing didn't have much time to reap the benefits of the new Oceanside. Jacob Heyman died at the age of 66 on May 13, 1904 in his home on California Street. His obituaries paid him tribute for his role in creating Carville.[11]

Changing public perceptions proved slow work. In 1905, the *San Francisco Call* still felt it had to remind its readers that "[t]hose places that are designated as suburbs and named 'Sunnyside,' 'Richmond,' 'Carville,' etc., are in the city and county of San Francisco."[12]

Not everyone was enamored with the name change and developments in the neighborhood. Some residents saw the introduction of electricity, gas service, and rising lot prices (quoted as high as $1,000-$1,500 in 1907) as ruining the spirit of Carville. The appearance of new conventional homes was noted as being "far from being a thing of beauty," and the desire for a rustic car house getaway didn't abate with the building of these homes.[13]

In January 1906, *Four Track News* informed would-be settlers that while old horse cars were no longer available, new car residences could be "constructed of well-made cable- and trolley-cars, perfectly sound and in good condition for habitation," and the United Railroads advertised that same month that it had early-generation electric car bodies for sale, "suitable for use in Carville."[14]

In addition to Oceanside, "Ozonia" was proposed as a new name for Carville. Likely inspired by L. Frank Baum's popular "Oz" fantasy books for children, it never caught on. [15]

City Services

The city recognized the need for a public school in Carville in 1902, but the Board of Education felt that until streets were improved, or at least *created* in the district it was useless to start construction. So, with 26 pupils, the Carville or Oceanside School opened in John Brumund's grocery store on the corner of 48th Avenue and Irving Street on March 23, 1903.

The children roamed the dunes at recess, and for a month of perfect attendance were granted an hour to play in Golden Gate Park.

In 1908, the Oceanside received a proper school building on 43rd Avenue between Irving and Judah streets. The school was so swamped by shifting dunes that an extra $3,000 had to be allocated soon after to put in a basement and retaining wall. This school later became Francis Scott Key Elementary School.

After years of lobbying for water mains and fire protection, the Oceanside welcomed Chemical Engine Company #12 in a new firehouse built on 45th Avenue in 1910.

The need for a fire station in the neighborhood had been made more than evident when another form of unusual dwelling caught fire and almost took most of Carville with it.

Dennis O'Brien lived in a former water tank tower on 48th Avenue between Irving and Judah streets (possibly the large one Jacob Heyman erected). The tank offered grand views of the ocean over the Great Highway berm, and O'Brien's house may have been one of the sturdiest structures in the area.

On the evening of April 20, 1901, a pot of lard over-boiled on his stove and the water-tower house caught fire. Because Carville didn't have any piped-in water, pressure hoses, or modern fire-fighting equipment, O'Brien's tower was totally destroyed. The adjoining house was heavily damaged and barely saved by a bucket brigade.[16]

Detail of the aerial photo on page 121. The three-wing building at upper left is the Oceanside School, opened in 1908, and the large two-story white building on the lower right is Chemical Engine Company #12, facing west on 45th Avenue, and opened in 1910. A lonely car house is still hunkered in the dunes between them.

Pioneer Grocers

John Brumund and Carl Barta were partners in a saloon on Polk Street in the 1890s before opening an establishment in Carville. Their *Villa Miramar* on Great Highway at Irving Street advertised itself as a "Wheelmen's Rest" to lure in the hoards of weekend bicyclists, but the owners quickly found out that they could also sell supplies to the community growing around them.

Barta died relatively soon after establishing the Villa Miramar, but his widow kept the business going, while Brumund split off to open his own store just to the east.

The businesses were soon joined by A.E. Harnish's market on the last block of Judah Street, run for a time by Louis Emetsberg and Fernando Cortez Ruggles. All three establishments acted not only as grocery and dry goods stores, but also as meeting and lodging places, post offices, and real estate rental agencies.

Demonstrating the topographical vagaries of the area, the Barta family was evicted from their business in 1907 after it was found that the Villa Miramar stood in the middle of what maps identified as 49th Avenue (today's La Playa Street).

Opposite: The Villa Miramar, advertising phone service about 1901. A young couple enjoy a cold beverage in front of A.E. Harnish's with car houses visible in the background.

Above: The extended Ruggles and Emetsberg families pose in front of the market at 4314-4316 Judah Street. Some of the family lived in the "real" house to the left.

The Big Shake-up

Clarence E. Judson took a swim in the cold surf at Ocean Beach every morning at 5:00 a.m. This was part of what drew Judson and his family out to Oceanside. How many men could take an invigorating dip in the roaring surf before work every day? Judson was a mechanic with the United Railroads. Rather than a car house, his family—a wife and three children—lived in a conventional home on 47th Avenue. After repairing street cars at work all day Judson likely didn't want to face the same job at home, and domiciles made of street cars were generally a bit cramped.

Myrtie Dickson's family lived just a couple of blocks from the Judsons. After starting with a five-street-car dwelling, with a stable and windmill for water, the family moved into a "real house" on 47th Avenue between Judah and Kirkham streets in October 1905.

On the morning of April 18, 1906 at 5:12 a.m., a violent shaking of her new home roused Myrtie from sleep. She got out of bed and immediately fell to the floor in the swaying. She described it later as being "a grip, just like a grip."

At the same time, Clarence Judson had just entered the ocean for his daily swim. A strange breaker took him off his feet, and he staggered toward the shore when "instantly there came such a shock I was thrown to my knees." Judson kept trying to stand and kept being thrown to the sand and surf, "getting tossed about by the breakers, my ears full of salt water and about a gallon in my stomach."

The mechanic fought and finally got out of the water, but the heaving dunes tossed him down repeatedly as he ran to his clothes and got dressed. "I reeled and staggered like a drunken man. I thought of wife and babies. I had left them asleep. I realized we had just had a terrible earthquake."

Judson ran back to his house and, while crossing the recently paved Great Highway, he noticed huge cracks. At the summit of the berm, he saw in Carville "houses were out of plumb, men, women and children were coming out in the streets, dogs were barking and chickens cackling."

La Boheme, the musicians' horse car clubhouse, had tipped up by a short end, causing everything inside to crash in a pile. Only the flagpole on "Mount Diablo" remained erect.

Myrtie Dickson tried to call friends downtown, but the lines were out. Telephone poles tilted at wild angles down Irving Street.

Unlike proverbial houses built on sand, most Carville buildings had survived. Those made of street cars, built to rumble up and down city hills, rattled, but remained intact. Other houses in the area were wood-framed, not the masonry and stone structures susceptible to failure in earthquakes. Neighborhood buildings swayed with the tremors, and some shifted or tilted from their foundations, but they didn't collapse.

After one of North America's strongest recorded earthquakes, losses were relatively minimal in Oceanside. At the Dickson house a lamp fell off a three-cornered table and broke, and the garage doors split open between the foundation and the house. Along with the skinned knees Myrtie got from falling out of bed, the damages were light.

Streetcar service on Lincoln Way stopped, as the tracks warped and were buried in shifting dunes. With the phone lines down, residents were cut off from the rest of the city. Myrtie Dickson's grandmother saw light and smoke in the east and told Myrtie perhaps she ought to go to the store and buy some provisions.

When Clarence Judson saw "vast columns of smoke" in the distance he "knew there were bad times in town."[17]

Telephone poles askew on 48th Avenue.

Cable cars used as temporary housing for refugees on Sutter Street.

"Had [the fire department] failed in this, their last effort, there would not be a house standing in San Francisco at the present writing save a few shacks south of the park or in the vicinity of Carville." [18]

Return of the Phoenix

Downtown and south of Market Street, the earthquake collapsed buildings, trapping people inside. Chimneys fell across town; street car lines warped, and precious water mains broke. Devastating fires began in different locations, joining into a large storm of destruction. Thousands fled the fires, some not stopping until they hit the ocean's edge.

The first people to reach Carville had limited, garbled news of fires and collapsed hotels, looting, and rumors of worse. Newspaper editor Fremont Older and his wife Cora abandoned their home downtown to sleep, or try to sleep, inside Mrs. Gunn's restaurant. Talk of an impending tidal wave went around the neighborhood and for two nights most of Carville's population and the newly-arrived refugees kept their distance from the beach by camping in the dunes.[19]

The fires continued raging into April 19 and 20. With assistance from a member of the National Guard, the artistic group *Les Jeunes* had one last toast at Coppa's before flames gutted the Montgomery Block. The studios of the artists, and much of Sutro's great library inside, succumbed to the holocaust as the area was reduced to skeletal ashes and blackened crags.

When the flames were finally extinguished after three terrible days, more than five miles of the city's core — North Beach, South of Market, the Financial District, Russian Hill, and Telegraph Hill — lay destroyed. Some 3,000 San Franciscans had lost their lives, and more than 225,000 suddenly found themselves homeless. Many left the city immediately. Others searched for shelter in the unburned parts of town or camped outside in the streets, empty lots, piers, or city parks.

Jack London traveled down from Sonoma with his wife and described the scene for *Collier's* magazine:

> San Francisco is gone. Nothing remains of it but memories and a fringe of dwelling-houses on its outskirts. Its industrial section is wiped out. Its business section is wiped out. Its social and residential section is wiped out. The factories and warehouses, the great stores and newspaper buildings, the hotels and the palaces of the nabobs, are all gone.[20]

With its financial core and most of its old neighborhoods destroyed, many agreed with Jack London's assessment. Surely, the population would disperse to seek shelter and employment across the bay in Oakland or up the coast in Portland, Oregon. Even rebuilt, it would lose its standing as a major city. San Francisco was gone for good.

But San Francisco, like the mythical phoenix on the city's flag, had risen from ashes before. The town had six major fires in the two years after its establishment in the 1850s, and each time it was rebuilt bigger and stronger. This instance would be no different.

Left: An earthquake refugee cottage moved to 47th Avenue in the Oceanside.

Below: Camp Richmond, a "cottage camp" on today's Park-Presidio Boulevard, operated from 1906 to 1908.

New Blood

Relief camps for the thousands burned out of their homes started with tents set up in parks and empty lots, but quickly became formalized communities run in military fashion. Over 5,000 small redwood cottages or "shacks" were built for the displaced, providing employment and keeping much of the city's workforce in town. When the camps closed in 1907 and 1908, many refugees took relief cottages with them, cobbling together two or three to create more permanent dwellings.

Refugee shack homes fit in quite well in the former Carville, where joining together odd little structures was routine. A number of the little shacks came to Oceanside, hauled by horse wagon across Golden Gate Park from Camp Richmond, one of the largest refugee camps.

The dislocation of thousands of San Franciscans, with people seeking homes of any kind outside of the fire zone, meant another population spurt for the former car colony by the ocean. Many who had rented cars as weekend or vacation getaways moved in permanently after their primary homes were destroyed.[21]

Car houses also made a comeback. Not only were thousands of people searching for shelter of any kind, but the disaster created a supply of new building stock for the unusual structures.

For decades, San Francisco beautification advocates had tenaciously, and in most cases successfully, fought against the unsightly overhead wires that electric street cars required, thereby keeping many cable car lines alive. The anxious frenzy to rebuild the city after the 1906 disaster eliminated resistance to such niceties. Also, most of the cable car rolling stock had been incinerated in the fire. If new cars had to be built, it made sense to have them be modern electric ones.

In May 1906, overhead wires appeared on Market Street for the first time as the transit companies transitioned to electricity. The Presidio and Ferries Company replaced its combination line of horse car, steam dummy, and cable car with electric cars in 1907. The United Railroads cut its cable car trackage in half between 1907 and 1908.[22] Suddenly more obsolete stock was on the market, ready for desperate home-seekers and the entrepreneurial to create quick domiciles. Even some electric cars became available to Carvillian house builders as wood car bodies made way for new steel cars.[23]

Just when it appeared the last vestiges of Carville were to be subsumed by conventional homes, the great disaster of 1906 created both an acute housing shortage and a stockpile of obsolete cars to meet the need.

Carville once more drew in story-seeking journalists. On March 15, 1908, both the *San Francisco Chronicle* and the *San Francisco Call* featured large Carville articles with color artwork and photos.

Chronicle writer Emmet O'Brien highlighted the growing divide between Oceansiders and Carvillians, and gloomily predicted the end of car house living while at the same time noting how car architecture style influenced more conventional shingled structures in regard to projections, elevations, window placement, and alignment. New homes, a population boom, and the increasing frequency of loud automobiles on the Ocean Boulevard were signs to O'Brien that Carville's charms were almost at an end.[24]

The advent of the auto made the area more accessible. The Oceanside seemed less like the country and more like a city neighborhood when one could drive there on new roads in a matter of minutes.

Another harbinger of change was the transition of Mrs. Patriarch's Vista del Mar from a country bed-and-breakfast to St. Andrews-by-the-Sea, a Protestant Episcopal Church.

The ladies auxiliary of St. Andrew's hosted a musicale at Oceanside Hall in November 1908.[25] Whether the drunken musicians of the *La Boheme* clubhouse took part is unrecorded, but it seems unlikely.

"...the resident who has a front platform for his parlor and a rear platform for his kitchen is no longer a welcome neighbor in the shifting sands."

—Emmet O'Brien
1908

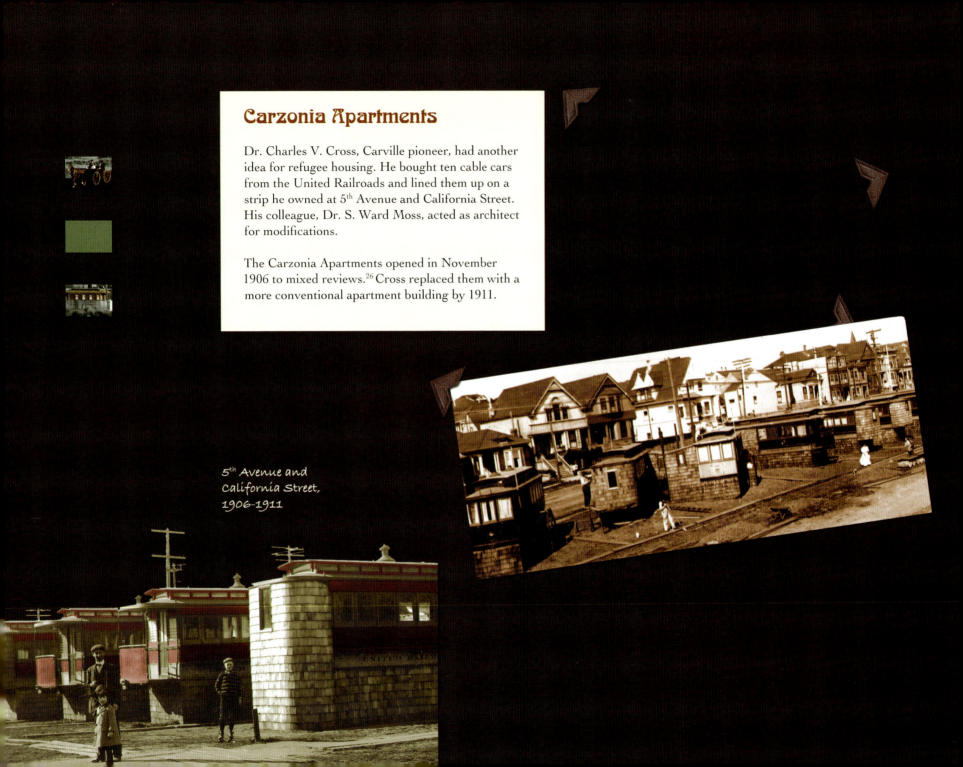

Carzonia Apartments

Dr. Charles V. Cross, Carville pioneer, had another idea for refugee housing. He bought ten cable cars from the United Railroads and lined them up on a strip he owned at 5th Avenue and California Street. His colleague, Dr. S. Ward Moss, acted as architect for modifications.

The Carzonia Apartments opened in November 1906 to mixed reviews.[26] Cross replaced them with a more conventional apartment building by 1911.

5th Avenue and California Street, 1906-1911

"The Property owners in the neighborhood are very much annoyed, as they consider them a disgrace..."[27]
—The Richmond Banner

Older and the Dynamiters

After the 1906 earthquake, *San Francisco Bulletin* editor Fremont Older and his wife Cora continued to rent a car beside Mrs. Gunn's restaurant. Older frequently retreated to Oceanside to swim in the ocean and relax after work, and it was there that assassins planned for him to die.

Corruption infested San Francisco city government in the early 20th century and it was an open secret that bribery and payoffs were part of doing business in the city before the earthquake and fire. Fremont Older was an editor of the crusading persuasion, and foresaw in the massive rebuilding of San Francisco a terrible opportunity for graft on a massive scale. He also imagined in the unsettled moment a chance to change the political climate.

Backed by Rudolph Spreckels, a reform-minded millionaire, Older quickly launched a campaign to expose the political machine that ran San Francisco. The federal government assigned a special prosecutor, indictments were issued, and the resulting "Graft Trials" became high theater in 1906 and 1907, with the *Bulletin* making the proceedings front page news.

Because of his active role in attacking the machine, Older received anonymous death threats from the criminal underworld. As a longtime newspaper editor, Older was used to such threats, and took them lightly.

It became harder to ignore the danger, however, when the prosecution's star witness, former supervisor James Gallagher, had his home dynamited.

A believer in redemption, Older had befriended and aided many former criminals and rough types when they needed a job or other help to reform. One of those friends passed Older with a whispered warning on the street: "Keep away from the beach."[28]

The editor refused to be cowed. He continued to visit his Carville cottage and Mrs. Gunn's restaurant but took the precaution of bringing plain-clothes policemen with him.

When the perpetrators of the Gallagher explosion were eventually arrested they revealed that they had also targeted Older. The dynamiters had gotten as far as storing explosives in the car next to Mrs. Gunn's before the presence of the bodyguards scared the would-be assassins off the job.[29]

The Graft Trials ended anticlimactically with only the purported leader of the political machine, Abe Ruef, doing any time. In the end, Older felt Ruef was mostly a scapegoat. After excoriating him for years, the fiery editor later published the former boss's memoirs in the *Bulletin* and lobbied for his release from prison.

Carville House where Padovres and the Claudianos tried to dynamite us

No. 5 OVERLAND MONTHLY Vol. LII
Founded 1868 — Bret Harte
San Francisco

AN EXCLUSIVE NEIGHBORHOOD IN CARVILLE.

IN A CARVILLE COURTYARD.

A CITY OF CARS
BY GIBBS ADAMS

San Francisco, a city of distinctive features, boasts none more unique than her quaint suburb of Carville by the Sea.

WITH SUCH A GARDEN AT THE FRONT DOOR ALL THE YEAR AROUND, WHO WOULD NOT LIVE IN AN OLD STREET CAR?

paradise of the clerk and small business man, who can daily enjoy a morning plunge in the invigorating breakers, yet

mania, a tough and wiry perennial flourishing alike in wind or flood or dr— The fragrant golden lu—

In the November 1908 issue of the Overland Monthly, Gibbs Adams estimated the area's population at some two thousand souls, "with its own stores, restaurants, churches, hotel, its artistic settlement, its colony of prominent musicians from the city, and best of all, its quaint homes, real yet of almost nominal cost." 31

Burning the Car Out of Carville

On June 3, 1913, the last horse car rumbled down a San Francisco street. A four-block spur connecting Sutter Street line passengers with the Ferry Building had been required by an expiring franchise agreement to be powered "by animal." Mayor James Rolph ceremonially held the reins on the last run. The era of true horse-powered public transit had finally and completely ended.

Remnants of Carville had become a tourist attraction, listed in the 1913 San Francisco Blue Book under "Points of Interest."[32] The clash between those who visited the beach and points of interest (and perhaps raise a little hell) and those who moved to Oceanside to have a quiet home intensified with improved roads and the growing popularity of automobiles.

Paved boulevards and horseless carriages injected new life into the roadhouses at the beach, and the 20th century version of "sporting men" could do the circuit in a night: drinking, carousing, and racing their autos on the Great Highway.

In 1912, the riotous behavior became so bad that Oceanside women, newly empowered with the right to vote in California, attempted to recall a police judge who repeatedly lowered the bail of accused rapists. The women came together because "now and then a decent mother of a family out there has been called from bed to take in a girl, sobbing, shamed, left half-stripped by the highway."[33]

Around this time Adolph Sutro's complicated estate was finally settled, and the blocks of sand where Colonel Dailey created his estate of driftwood, where Carville originated, was slated for new development.

The Oceanside Improvement Club saw an opportunity to make a statement.

Residents wanted Oceanside recognized as a real neighborhood, with families and churches and businessmen trying to make honest livings. But to many, Carville represented licentiousness, bohemian idleness, and "petting parties" in automobiles. Now, in response, the Oceanside Improvement Club proposed to "burn the car out of Carville."

On July 4, 1913, with the permission of Sutro's daughter, the organization made a bonfire on block 624. Four cars, including the old Falcons clubhouse, went up in flames. The improvement club publicized a cumbersome but unambiguous slogan for the event: "Make clean today by sweeping and burning up the debris of yesterday."[34]

The occasion drew hundreds of people. To make it more of an Independence Day celebration and less of a funeral, Alexander Russell, now acting president of the club, tossed $10 of fireworks into the bonfire.

Before their old clubhouse was incinerated, Mr. and Mrs. Fitzgerald recalled for a San Francisco Chronicle reporter all the famous people that had visited or dined with the Falcons over the previous 18 years.

Some names quoted were likely, while others were patently impossible.

Roadhouses

Roadhouses proliferated at Ocean Beach in the 1910s and 1920s with the arrival of autos and newly paved roads. In addition to the venerable Cliff House, the old Oceanside House returned as a bar and restaurant called Tait's-at-the-Beach.

Other establishments offering liquor and meals to pleasure seekers included Baby Smith's, the Surf, the M&M, Uncle Tom's Cabin, Mike Sheehan's, the Three Aces, the Breakers, the Canary Cottage, Somerset's, Shorty Roberts' Sea Breeze and Roberts-at-the-Beach, Dibble's, and Murray's.

"For along that highway that borders the ocean are certain lawless resorts; along that highway, late at night, there are wild sounds of revel from speeding automobiles, and sometimes there are bitter cries from drunken, dazed, betrayed women." [35]

THE ORIGINAL ROBERTS AT THE BEACH SEABREEZE RESORT IN 1897. SAN FRANCISCO

Somerset's Road House Great Highway Ocean Beach 1910.

Good-byes

After the burning, Carville didn't immediately disappear. Mary Gunn, whose tea room of two old horse cars had hosted men and women of power and prestige, stayed in business until her death in 1923. Her obituary mentioned that after she took ill, many waited "for the shades [of her restaurant] to go up," but iconoclast Mrs. Gunn would "never again raise those tattered shades."[36]

Many cars melted into the neighborhood, hidden in framework, shingled or spackled invisible. The less camouflaged car houses, mostly unmodified rentals, were left to get seedy by landlords. Jules Getz who let out a row of street cars into the 1920s, admitted the cars "were not in good repute."[37]

Ida Russell died in 1917 after she underwent a bizarre beauty treatment to remove wrinkles from her throat. The beautician applied a solution that included carbolic acid and the combination of the acid and a physician's morphine injection (for pain relief) ended the life of the robust 60-year-old woman.[38] Her husband Alexander, he who burned the car out of Carville, sold his home in 1919. The rambling structure reverted to its original use as a roadhouse, this time named Tait's-at-the-Beach. After wobbling through Prohibition and the Depression, the landmark "House of Mystery" burned down in a suspicious fire in 1940.[39]

A relative of the author poses in front of Mrs. Gunn's with a friend, circa 1920.

Tait's-at-the-Beach

Sunset Emergence

Fueled by a booming economy, home building operations moved onto the great sand dunes in the 1920s. Using assembly-line techniques, family-run companies such as the Standard Building Company (Carl and Fred Gellert) and Henry Doelger Company thrived constructing rows of simple but sturdy houses.

The typical house was two or three bedrooms elevated over a garage and pressed up against its neighbors, as the builders maximized the land value by stuffing as many houses on a block as possible. Minimal attention was paid to exterior decoration, which was usually stucco: perhaps an appliquéed medallion, a stippled pattern, or a shaped parapet. The buildings were just different enough, in the words of one writer, "that if you happened to arrive home a few sheets to the wind on a fog-heavy night, you could still pick yours out."[40]

The Great Depression of the 1930s strangely didn't slow the pace of construction. The federal government practically paid companies to build, hoping to keep the industry alive. Federal Housing Administration loans were easy for buyers to obtain and the builders themselves offered deals to get rid of inventory. Thousands of renters purchased their first homes on the developing west side of San Francisco.

New stucco homes march across the dunes around 30th Avenue and Pacheco Street in the 1930s.

Disparate neighborhoods, all with different names, grew closer, knit together, as the vast sand dunes separating them disappeared under a carpet of stucco homes and concrete. "Oceanside" began to fade in use as the city's new super district, everything from Golden Gate Park south to Sloat Boulevard, became the "Sunset District."

When servicemen returned from World War II, ready to buy homes and start families with easy government financing, the Sunset boomed into a solidly middle class neighborhood of respectable families living in modest tract housing.

Not everyone was impressed. Critics attacked the architecture and the homogenous population of "the Avenues." Once considered a foggy wasteland of sand dunes, the Sunset District was now, to some, a foggy wasteland of cookie-cutter homes and conformist nuclear families.

Every so often stories bubbled up remembering Carville and its raucous community of bohemians at the beach. Rumors were swapped of old street cars still hidden away, rented cheaply in backyards or secreted in second floors.

That such a place might be in the bland Sunset made the whole story more surprising and intriguing.

Henry Doelger Company advertisement, 1941.

Opposite page and left: Outer Sunset in the 1910s and 1930s.

"[The] Sunset may be [San Francisco's] only neighborhood without a trace of apparent charm or history; a vast, drab tract of stucco homes sloping down to the sea." [41]

Carville to Real Homes

The real estate firm of Baldwin & Howell became the selling agent for Adolph Sutro's estate when probate ended in the 1910s The company recognized the romance of the old car village while at the same time assuring potential buyers the days of car houses had passed. The firm hopefully headlined a sales brochure "From Carville to Real Homes."

A map in the brochure promised a new electric street car line (never built), and depicted the Oceanside neighborhood with imaginary garden courtyards, flourishing trees, and ridiculously large homes.

Fanciful map and new street car line aside, the pamphlet promoted the same attractions that drew the first Carville residents: "You can run to the beach in your bathing suit."[42]

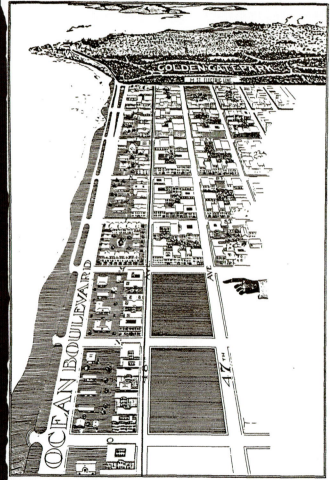

A franchise has been granted for an electric line down 48th Avenue,

TERMS

$50 Down $10 Per Month

Prices range from
$500
Upwards

No lots of less than 25 foot frontage with varying depths of from 90 to 120 ft.

Rapid Transit
25 minutes to center of City

Invigorating Climate
Best in the State

No Ferry Trip
Wife Won't Worry

Right on the Ocean
Fishing—Bathing—Beach for the Babies

Baldwin & Howell
Sales Agents

318-324 Kearny Street
San Francisco, California

ACT 5

Car Extinction

"During my trekking up and down 47th, 48th, and the Great Highway, looking for the elusive remnant Carville cable cars, I was amazed by the number of people who never heard

Treasure Hunting

From the 1930s on, the story of Carville reappeared in newspapers and magazines about every seven to ten years. Reporters and columnists stumbled upon, and cribbed from, the work of their predecessors and a standard, somewhat accurate, narrative was set:

1) Eccentric and/or impoverished settlers, maybe refugees from the 1906 Earthquake and Fire, found a junk yard of old cars at the beach and moved in.

2) Residents burned Carville to make way for a new respectable neighborhood.

3) There are a few Carville homes hiding in the dull fabric of the Sunset District.

In 1934, the *San Francisco News* profiled John Morehead, 76 years old, living with his niece Rita Curran, in a six-car house at 1439 47th Avenue. Like the original Carville residents, Morehead proudly used beach driftwood for firewood and coal oil lamps for lighting.[2]

The *News* returned to the Carville story in 1947 in a three-part series on the Sunset District. At the time, San Francisco's last cable car routes were under heavy pressure to be replaced by buses. The *News* noted that cable cars would never be extinct from San Francisco as long as Carville homes survived.[3]

San Francisco Chronicle columnist Robert O'Brien remembered Carville in a 1950 column focusing on the Falcons Bicycle Club car, which he called a "Bedouin retreat." Edwin Emerson replied to O'Brien's article with his personal memories of the Fuzzy Bunch car, listing every well-known member of San Francisco's *fin de siecle* Bohemia, and naming Dr. Charles V. Cross as their benefactor.[4] The next decade, columnist Millie Robbins composed a whole Carville cycle across three days: Colonel Dailey, the Lady Falcons, and the Burning of Carville.[5]

In 1964, Margot Patterson Doss wrote in the *Chronicle* that looking for Carville homes was akin to being an archeologist, as "time, affluence and adroit carpentry" had hidden away the car houses.

She and her photographer did the rounds, visiting the old Fitzgerald house on 47th Avenue, a car apartment occupied by Ken Malucelli, and a home farther south on 47th Avenue with two horse cars on the second floor. Doss noted the general eccentricity of beach life and implied the pioneers of Carville were poor but inventive.[6]

1208 48th Avenue, near Lincoln Way.

1372 48th Avenue, near Judah Street.

1608 48th Avenue (Old Roy Andrus home).

Police Officer Jesse Brown Cook, an enthusiastic hobby photographer, wandered the streets of Oceanside in 1925, capturing on film as many visible car houses as he could find.

"No rent necessary for these poor tenants. At last we have met a landlord who is taking care of the needy and gives them rental free when they can't offer to pay. The landlord is Jules Getz of San Francisco who owns a huge number of street car homes. These street cars when fitted up neatly make ideal home for the poor and needy. They are located in the Sunset district, San Francisco." [7]

— P & A Photos Caption,
January 8, 1924

Ken's Cottage

Ken Malucelli, an actor and singer, appreciated a unique place with cheap rent. In 1962, he read a newspaper advertisement for a rear cottage behind a set of conventional flats at 1352-1354 48th Avenue. The rent was a very reasonable $45 a month.

A California Street-style cable car made up the main section of the apartment. Additions at either end created a small breakfast nook and a back bedroom. A bathroom had been installed in one end of the car. The built-in benches had been removed. The ventilator windows in the roof were reglazed with wavy amber glass, but still let in the afternoon sun.

Ken moved in with his partner Dennis, who painted the whole cottage fire-engine red. When they broke up, Ken's new boyfriend Cliff "decided to erase Dennis by repainting the car all yellow."

Ken moved out in 1964, but still has fond memories of the little cottage. No sign of the car house is apparent today and Ken believes it was demolished years ago.

Ken Malucelli in 2007.

Car house behind 1354 48th Avenue, early 1960s.

1415 47th Avenue

Ida Fitzgerald, leader of the Falcons Bicycling Club, and her husband Robert, Superior Court clerk and first president of the Oceanside Improvement Club, loved car houses. The couple rented two of the first four cars in the old Sutro section of Carville, and built their own near the corner of 47th Avenue and Judah Street in the first years of the 20th century.

On the second floor of 1415 47th Avenue the Fitzgeralds joined two horse cars, with a sidewall from each removed, creating one large room. Where the two ribbed roofs met, taller people had to duck. In 1930, when the childless couple had been married over fifty years, they hit hard times financially and made a public plea for donations to keep their cherished car house.[8]

The unique interior of the second floor was still in place in 1947 when Mrs. Viola Adams and her daughter Ann Marie escorted reporters through the house. When Frank Lemus bought it with his wife in 1961 the ribbed ceilings and horse car interiors had been removed, and the Lemuses had no idea of the building's vehicular past.

After a century of existence the house is a hodge-podge of paneling and closed window frames as surrounding construction has blocked views. It is an interesting, quirky place, a product of handyman work over decades. Once shingled, the building is now clad with aluminum siding.

Looking east out of the same checkerboard wall of windows Miss Ann Marie Adams posed in front of in 1947, one can feel through the carpeting a ridge where the horse car frames end and the front addition begins.

1415 47th Avenue in 2007.

Left: Part of the top floor of 1415 47th Avenue in 1947. Some time in the 1950s the two horse cars were removed to create a flat ceiling. Frank Lemus (below) bought the home in 1961.

Mrs. Suggs' House

Mr. and Mrs. Charles F. Suggs lived behind the Coliseum Theater in the Richmond District at 330 Ninth Avenue. They had inherited the house from Mrs. Suggs' sister, and moved in when she died in 1941. By the early 1960s, Charles Suggs had also passed away, and at that time Mrs. Suggs accepted an offer from the City of San Francisco to purchase her home. A citywide project to create small municipal parking lots was underway and 330 Ninth Avenue had to make way for "Clement Shopper's Parking Center No. 2."

During demolition it was discovered that the simple house turned out to be made of three United Railroads cable car trailers, cleverly enmeshed together decades earlier by Mrs. Suggs' brother-in-law, Charlie Hulse, who was known as an "imaginative handycraftsperson." His granddaughter in 2007 remembered years of playing in the Suggs house and never suspecting its transportational past.

The *San Francisco Chronicle* and other media came out to report on the odd structure and stories of Carville again made the rounds.[9]

"For years it was a little-known fact that the humble, asbestos-shingled structure at 330 Ninth avenue was, in reality, three pre-quake horse-drawn street cars, cleverly joined and roofed over to make a cozy abode." [10]
— San Francisco Chronicle

Above and opposite: Backyard car houses photographed by transit historian Richard Schlaich in the 1960s. The horse car on opposite page was rescued from its use as a tool shed and restored for service and display in San Jose's Kelly Park.

End Days

Natalie Jahraus Cowan wrote perhaps the most thorough and accurate article on Carville for *California History* in 1978. Working as a librarian at the California Historical Society, she had at hand the resources and research skills to uncover photographs, scrapbooks, and stories on the community. In her article, Jahraus suggested it was likely that cars were still hiding in the old Oceanside.[11]

The next year Margot Patterson Doss returned to write about Carville and again led off with her theory that the community emerged out of a trash heap:

> [Carville] began as a junkyard—a cluster of outmoded street cars, electric line cars, horse-drawn cars, dinkies and cable cars that had been hauled out H street to the beach and left in the dunes for the elements to dismantle.[12]

Doss revisited the Fitzgerald house and the car home fifty feet to the south, interviewing old timers about wells, chicken coops, and wacky neighbors who flew chamber pots from flagpoles. (Former 46th Avenue resident Bob Herbert remembered there were so many characters on his block that his mother called it "Dingbat Row.")

By this time the area had regained some of its old unsavory reputation. The beach drew surfers and dog walkers, but also wandering alcoholics and teens drag racing on the Great Highway. Many hippies and other counter-culture types moved into the beachside cottages, and one newspaper summed up the area with an article headlined "Ocean Beach—Dingy But Delightful." The reporter assured his readers that "Ocean Beach is only half full of creeps."[13]

Many of the early Oceanside cottages became rental properties, and received minimal maintenance. Corrosive salt air and modernist trends stripped away original decorative elements as owners slapped on asbestos shingles, stucco, faux stone, or vinyl siding. Various real estate booms and housing shortages in San Francisco brought speculators who demolished cottages for large multiple-unit buildings, a practice which continues today.

In the face of a full century of real estate pressures, negligent landlords, indifferent tenants, changing tastes, and an almost carnivorous fog, it seemed very unlikely any Carville home could see the light of the 21st century.

At least one has…

Survivor

1632 Great Highway doesn't call attention to itself. One writer has described the building as "a shingled box with aluminum frame windows."[14] This box may be the last Carville house in San Francisco.

In 1908, Mrs. Minnie V. Collins bought the ocean-fronting lot at 1632 Great Highway, between Lawton and Moraga streets. There she had two cable cars and a horse car joined together and raised on a frame. The interior walls of the cable cars were removed and parts of the roofs raised to create a spacious living room. The horse car, left mostly intact, complete with sliding door, served as a small bedroom. The back quarter of the cars, she transformed into a kitchen and dining area. An enclosed porch on the ocean and street-facing side of the structure made for a nice place to take in sunsets; at least it did, Mrs. Collins would complain, until the city elevated the berm of the Great Highway and obstructed her view of the ocean.[15]

Minnie Collins owned and lived in the house until at least 1947, when she was interviewed by a reporter. In the 1970s, a new owner, David A. Lyon, restored much of the structure and removed part of the back kitchen to partition and sell the lot next door.

In 1997, filmmaker Scott Anderson purchased 1632 Great Highway. Mr. Anderson has much in common with the first Carville residents. He works in a creative field as an Academy Award-winning visual effects designer, and often rents his unique house to surfers, Web designers, and others who would feel at home with the bohemian originators of Carville. Like many in the neighborhood, he was drawn to the area for the beach, being a surfer himself.

Anderson knows what a jewel he owns and his responsibilities to its uniqueness: "If indeed mine is the very last one, it's a resource that almost slipped away without anyone knowing it existed."

Keeping up the maintenance and trying to preserve three antique cars formed into one historic home is difficult. "I'm trying to do the best I can to keep it in the state it is."

Much of the historical fabric remains. One wall has the wooden benches of the old cable car still built in, where one can recline where passengers in the 1890s sat, under the original tongue-and-groove slat ceiling. Glass lanterns, old kerosene lamps, hang over the space, and it doesn't take much to believe the room is about to rumble on a pair of rails through a Victorian street scene.

1632 Great Highway from the back, where the ends of two cable cars and part of a horse car are exposed.

Perhaps the last complete car house in San Francisco, 1632 Great Highway is made of two cable cars opened up to form a large living room, and one intact horse car that acts as a bedroom. A west side addition and ground-floor apartment complete the building.

Above: The front of the car house is set back from the street. Right: A graphic by Doug Stern shows how the cable cars are visible from the home's east and north sides.

Interior views of the unique home. Crowns of the cable cars are still visible in the attic.

A 2009 Walk on the West Side

The physical landscape of today's Outer Sunset is far different from its ancestral communities of Carville and Oceanside. The well-paved streets are lined with splintering wood telephone poles and parked automobiles. Views of the ocean are hidden by unbroken rows of houses and apartment buildings. In most of the neighborhood one has a better chance of smelling the sea than seeing or hearing it. There is less sand, more concrete, perhaps the same amount of fog.

While this corporeal, modern neighborhood doesn't resemble Carville, its *cultural* landscape burns with some of the same bohemian spirit possessed by its founders. Along the Great Highway, beach lovers have covered stucco façades with garish colors and murals that the *Les Jeunes* artists would appreciate.

Every morning at Java Beach Café, at La Playa and Judah streets, young women from Ireland froth up lattés for dog walkers while famished surfers, with salty reminders of the waves in their eyebrows, dig into oatmeal. Surfing, a sport (hobby? lifestyle?) that didn't exist in the 1890s, draws the same relaxed, life-luxuriating characters that would ride with the Falcon Bicycle Club. Many men and women—some with well-paying jobs, able to live anywhere they want in the expensive Bay Area—rent run-down apartments near the beach just for the opportunity to pull on a wetsuit after work and hit the waves. Java Beach is a cultural touchstone to the surfers and other residents of the area, much as Colonel Dailey's "coffee saloon" was to Carvillians.

The Cliff House up the road, and the Beach Chalet restaurant in Golden Gate Park draw in tourists and locals for a meal or a drink, although the clientele is more respectable than the men in fast cars that used to patronize Shorty Roberts' or the Canary Cottage.

And scanning the streetscapes of these outer avenues, one *can* imagine other Carville homes still hiding, perhaps even from their current owners or tenants. Long, boxy buildings hint of street car bones under lathe and shingles. While it is unlikely another intact car house like 1632 Great Highway exists, perhaps some publicity-shy individual is right now drinking tea in a Market Street Railway horse car, or napping peacefully on the bench of a California Street cable car.

And maybe after this book is published, when the story of Carville again makes the rounds, this treasure-hunting boy will be directed to a secret beachside jewel, and, in combination with a winning lottery ticket, he will buy his quirky *Wild Wild West* home.

Left: Great Highway house.
Above: Kirkham Street house; Java Beach Café.

Notes and Citations

For expanded notes and bibliography, as well as more photos, information, and stories of other car communities across the United States, visit www.carville-book.com.

Frequently used sources
SFBU   *San Francisco Bulletin*
SFCL   *San Francisco Call*
SFCH   *San Francisco Chronicle*
SFEX   *San Francisco Examiner*
SFNW   *San Francisco News*
TRAV   *The Traveler*

Introduction

1. John H. White, Jr., "Steam in the Streets: The Grice and Long Dummy," *Technology and Culture* 27, no. 1. (1986), 106-109.

2. George W. Hilton, *The Cable Car in America, A New Treatise upon Cable or Rope Traction as Applied to the Working of Street and Other Railways.* (Stanford: Stanford University Press, 1997), 15. "…the social costs of horse traction were the most offensive in the history of transportation."

3. Walter Rice, Ph.D., and Emiliano Echeverria, *When Steam Ran on the Streets of San Francisco,* (Forty Fort, PA: Harold E. Cox), 2002, 8-9.

4. Hilton, 23.

5. Rice, 9.

6. Today only three routes remain in the city, run by electric motors from the powerhouse. Generally filled with tourists, they play little role in taking commuters to work.

7. Emiliano Echeverria, and Walter Rice, PhD., "Why the Octopus Left the Streets of San Francisco," *Bay Area Electric Railroad Association Journal* 2 (Spring 2007), 11.

8. Spenser Masters, "The Market-Street System," *The Wave,* (12 March 1898), 4.

9. Echeverria, 17.

10. *Ibid,* 17.

Act 1
Origins of Carville's Building Stock

1. Labor problems eventually did Vining in. He was forced to resign after a successful carman's strike in 1902. Paul C. Trimble, "Richard Cornelius, Division 205 and the Great URR Strike of 1907," *Bay Area Electric Railroad Association Journal* 2 (Spring 2007), 26.

2. Echeverria, 11-13.

3. Flora Haines Loughead, "Street Car Homes," *TRAV,* (December 1898), 85.

4. "At the End of their Trip," *SFEX,* (22 September 1895,), 19. Also, Loughead, 85.

5. Juliet Wilbor Tompkins, "The Life Informal in California," *Outing* 41 (January 1903), 445. Laura B. Starr, "The Arks of Arktown, *The Strand* 18, (November 1899), 98. E.W., "Arking," *TRAV,* (April 1894), 66.

6. "At the End of their Trip," *SFEX,* 19.

7. *Ibid,* 19.

8. "A habitat of street cars," *SFEX,* (11 April 1895), 7.

9. Echeverria, 13.

10. "A Veritable Desert in the City of San Francisco," *SFCL,* (23 May 1897), 27.

11. "At the End of their Trip," *SFEX,* 19.

12. "The City's Suburbs — how San Francisco is spreading in many directions," *SFEX,* (9 September 1895), 4.

13. "At the End of their Trip," *SFEX,* 19.

14. Letter to Louis Sutro, November 7, 1885, California State Library, Sutro Branch, Sutro Manuscript Collection, Drawer 3. "A Barbecue in the Rain," *SFCL,* (3 February 1892), 7.

15. "Burn the Car out of 'Carville,'" *SFCL,* (6 July 1913), 38.

16. J.K., "Carville," *The Wave,* (11 September 1897), 4.

17. Millie Robbins, "Among the Rank and File," *SFCH,* (5 June 1963), 18. Similarly, the author's great-great-grandfather was known as "Colonel Slinkey" but never commanded anyone with a rank higher than hotel busboy.

18. "A Barbecue in the Rain," *SFCL*, (3 February 1892), 7.
19. Cora Older, "People Who Live in Cars," *SFBU*, (11 July 1896). Date of *City of New York* crash from James Delgado and Stephen Haller, *Shipwrecks at the Golden Gate*, (San Francisco: Lexikos), 1989.
20. "Quaint Village of Condemned Street Railway Cars on the Ocean Beach," *SFCH*, (4 October 1896). "Carville," *The Wave*, (11 September 1897), 4. Also, Older, "People Who Live in Cars."
21. Older, "People Who Live in Cars."
22. Rice, 27-37.
23. "A Holiday Scene by the Glad Sea Waves," *SFCL*, (2 August 1896), 19.
24. "Quaint Village of Condemned Street Railway Cars on the Ocean Beach," *SFCH*, (4 October 1896).
25. *TRAV*, (October 1894), 59.
26. "Facts, Fancies and Foibles," *TRAV*, (October 1894), 59.
27. Loughead, 85. Also, "Quaint Village of Condemned Street Railway Cars on the Ocean Beach," *SFCH*, (4 October 1896).
28. Tompkins, 447.
29. "Burn the Car out of 'Carville,'" *SFCL*, (6 July 1913), 38.
30. Loughead, 85.
31. *Ibid*, 85.
32. "Carville," *The Wave*, (11 September 1897), 4.

Act 2
Heymanville & How to Build a Car House

1. Jane Sudekum, "Sunset—Sandlot City," *SFNW*, (10 April 1947), 13. Real estate man Jules Getz quoted.
2. Agnes Foster Buchanan, "The Settlement of Carville, *Country Life in America* 11 (March 1907), 429.
3. Heyman advertisements from *SFCH*: (1 January 1899), 57; (19 February 1899), 28; (19 March 1899), 28; (4 June 1899), 29.
4. Gibbs Adams, "A City of Cars," *Overland Monthly* 52, no. 5, (November 1908), 399.
5. "The Oddest Suburban Town in America," *SFCL*, (23 July 1899), 31.
6. Buchanan, 431.
7. "The Oddest Suburban…" Other writers and reporters would continue to use the name "Cartown" for the whole community. In 1901, both *The Strand* and *Scientific American* used the name Cartown in large articles.
8. "Carville-By-The-Sea," *Washington Post*, (13 August 1899), 28. "Car Towns in Suburbs," *New York Sun*, (14 July 1901).
9. Sudekum, (10 April 1947), 13.
10. Sarah Comstock, "Carville," *Four Track News* 10, no. 1, (January 1906), 51.
11. Gelett Burgess and Will Irwin, *The Picaroons*, (New York: McClure, Phillips and Co., 1904), 154.
12. "Method of Utilizing Old Street Cars," *Scientific American* 84, (29 June 1901), 409.
13. Comstock, 51.
14. "Curiosities of Cartown," *New York Times*, (15 May 1904), SM8.
15. Tompkins, 447.
16. Email from Emiliano Echeverria to the author, February 5, 2008.
17. Loughead, 85.
18. Comstock, 51.
19. Buchanan, 431.
20. Adams, 402.
21. "Schooner Goes Ashore Over Grave of the Ship King Philip," *SFCL*, (14 March 1902), 12.
22. Adams, 401. Older's patronage is remembered in Evelyn Wells, *Fremont Older*, (New York: Appleton-Century, 1936), 176-177.
23. "The Man Who Lives Among Skeletons," *SFCL*, (5 January 1902), 5.
24. Leslie Gilliams, "Cartown," *The Strand*, 22, (November 1901), 576.
25. "Curiosities of Cartown," SM8.
26. Tompkins, 445.

Act 3
Haunt of Bohemia

1. Robert O'Brien, "Riptides," *SFCH*, (18 September 1950).
2. Comstock, 50.
3. Warren Unna and Bruce Rogers, *The Coppa Murals: a pageant of Bohemian life in San Francisco at the turn of the century*, (San Francisco: Book Club of California, 1952)
4. John Hamilton Gilmour, "Girl Socialist of San Francisco," *SFEX*, (3 October 1897), 10. O'Brien, "Riptides," *SFCH*, (18 September 1950).
5. O'Brien, "Riptides," *SFCH*, (18 September 1950).
6. *Ibid*.
7. Gelett Burgess, *Behind the Scenes: Glimpses of Fin de Siecle San Francisco*, with commentaries by Joseph M. Backus, (San Francisco: Book Club of California, 1968), 10. Elsie Whitaker Martinez, *San Francisco Bay Area writers and artists: an interview conducted by Franklin D. Walker and Willa Klug Baum*, (Berkeley: ROHO, 1969), 227. "Gelett Burgess in Odd Skins," *SFCL*, (11 May 1897), 9.
8. Burgess, *The Picaroons*, 143-155.
9. Gelett Burgess, *The Heart Line*, (Indianapolis: The Bobbs-Merrill Co., 1907), 128-129
10. Willard Huntington Wright, "Hotbed of Soulful Culture," *Los Angeles Times*, (22 May 1910).
11. Martinez, 227.
12. Waldemar Young, "'Light Summer Reading' Served Without The Slightest Effort To the Ready Rescue of the Tired Businessman," *SFCH*, (16 July 1910).
13. "Historic Poster on Sale," *SFCH*, (20 February 1978).
14. Alice Rix, "She Who Would Be a Bohemian," *SFEX*, (19 January 1896), 31.
15. Gilliams, 574.
16. Comstock, 51.
17. Rix, 31.
18. Comstock, 50.
19. "Bohemia in a Horse Car," *SFCL*, (15 March 1908), 3.
20. "Method of Utilizing Old Street Cars."
21. Albert Parry, *Garrets and Pretenders—A History of Bohemian America*, (New York: Dover Press, 1960), 235.
22. "Roar of Waves is His Requiem," *SFCL*, (15 October 1903), 3.
23. *Ibid*, 3.

Act 4
The Rise of Oceanside

1. Tompkins, 449.
2. *Ibid*, 448.
3. *SFCL*, (10 May 1903), 25; (15 March 1903), 23.
4. Brian and Hidemi Riggs, *House of Silent Light: the Dawning of Zen in Gilded Age America*, (Unpublished manuscript), 160. Quoting *SFEX*, (15 September 1910), 2.
5. *Ibid*, 3.
6. Rick Fields, *How the Swans Came to the Lake*, (Boston: Shambhala Publications, 1986), 169.
7. "Oceanside Improvement Club," *Sunset Journal*, (28 January 1910).
8. "Ocean Boulevard," *SFCL*, (3 May 1903), 35.
9. "Agrees to Light the 'Carville' District," *SFCL*, (11 December 1903), 7.
10. "More Buildings Are Condemned," *SFCL*, (8 April 1903). "Park Affairs are Discussed," *SFCL*, (9 May 1903).
11. "Death Calls a Well Known Realty Dealer," *SFCL*, (14 May 1904), 14.
12. *SFCL*, (18 November 1905), 8.
13. Buchanan, 435.
14. Comstock, 50. United Railroads ad: *SFCL*, (23 January 1906), 13.
15. Buchanan, 429.
16. "Fire Destroys Two Ocean Beach Houses," *SFCL*, (21 April 1901), 23.
17. "In the Surf at the Time of the Quake," *SFCH*, (24 May 1906) and Myrtie Dickson memories in Patricia A. Turner, *1906 Remembered*, (San Francisco: Friends of the San Francisco Public Library, 1981), 55-57.

18. "Great Fire Halted," *Oakland Tribune*, (20 April 1906), 1.
19. "In the Surf…" *SFCH*.
20. Jack London, "The Story of an Eyewitness," *Collier's*, (5 May 1906).
21. Adams, 402.
22. Trimble, 28, 33, 40.
23. Advertisement, *SFCH*, (23 January 1906), 13.
24. Emmett M. O'Brien, "The Odd City on Ocean Beach," *SFCH*, (15 March 1908), 12.
25. "Program, Bazaar and Musical Entertainment at Oceanside Hall," November 7, 1908, California State Library, Sutro Branch.
26. "Improvements and Additions," *The Richmond Banner*, (23 November 1906), 5. "Turns Old Street Cars into Modern Apartments," *SFCH*, (26 November 1906), 14. "Carzonia," *The Richmond Banner*, (4 January 1907), 4.
27. *The Richmond Banner*, (23 November 1906), 4.
28. Fremont Older, *My Own Story*, (San Francisco: Call Publishing Company, 1919), 85-86.
29. Cora Older, "The Story of a Reformer's Wife," *McClure's Magazine*, 33, (July 1909), 277-293.
30. Older, Fremont, 88.
31. Adams, 399.
32. *San Francisco Blue Book*, 1913, 19.
33. Miriam Michelson, "Vice and the Women's Vote," *Sunset, the Pacific Monthly*, (April 1913), 345.
34. "Burn the car out of Carville," *SFCH*, (6 July 1913), 38.
35. Michelson, 345.
36. "Tram 'Tea Room' of Mary Gunn Closed by Death," (25 May, 1923). Newspaper clipping from Cora Older Scrapbooks, California Historical Society.
37. Sudekum, 13.
38. Riggs, 179-182.
39. Woody LaBounty, "Tait's-at-the-Beach: The House of Mystery," August 2003. Western Neighborhoods Project Web site, accessed 15 January 2008. URL: http://www.outsidelands.org/sw21.php
40. Ken Garcia, "Visionary's 'ticky-tacky' Landmarks," *SFCH*, (15 October 2002).
41. Jennifer Reese, "Streetcar Suburb," *Preservation, the Magazine of the National Trust for Historic Preservation*, (Jan/Feb 1999).
42. Baldwin & Howell, "Ocean Boulevard Lots" brochure. California Historical Society, dating sometime between 1913 and 1917.

Act 5
Car Extinction

1. James L. Heisterkamp, "Scrapbook, Olden San Francisco, Carville and its Last Remnant," (Unpublished manuscript, 1996), 96. San Francisco History Center, San Francisco Public Library.
2. "Horse-Cars of 75 Years Ago Are Their Home," *SFNW*, (23 February 1934).
3. Jane Sudekum, "Sunset—Sandlot City," *SFNW*, (7-10 April 1947).
4. Robert O'Brien, "Riptides," *SFCH*, (11, 18 September 1950).
5. Millie Robbins, "Millie's Column," *SFCH*, (8-10 June 1963).
6. Margot Patterson Doss, "Walk Where the Horse Cars Went," *SFCH*, Bonanza Section, (December 6, 1964).
7. P& A News wire caption found on the back of photograph at California Historical Society.
8. "Face Dispossess Notice," *SFCH*, (4 December 1930), 2
9. Bob Robertson, "House Built of Horse Cars," *SFCH*? (Newspaper clipping from the history file in the San Francisco Public Library's Richmond branch. No date or newspaper identification.)
10. *Ibid*.
11. Natalie Jahraus Cowan, *California History 57* (Winter 1978/79).
12. Margot Patterson Doss, "San Francisco At Your Feet," *San Francisco Examiner & Chronicle*, Sunday Punch, (21 January 1979), 6.
13. Peter Stack, "Ocean Beach—Dingy But Delightful," *SFCH*, (5 September 1977), 5.
14. Reese, 53.
15. Jane Sudekum, "Sunset—Sandlot City," *SFNW*, (8 April 1947), 13.

Image Credits

Page 2: Postcard image of Carville home on the 1300 block of La Playa Street. Author's collection. Back of postcard sent by Mable Ruggles from Carville. Collection of Frank Sternad.

Page 6: "Carville at Ocean Beach." (Colorized by the author.) California History Section, California State Library, Sacramento, CA.

Page 8: U.S. Geological Survey Map, 1899. Author's collection.

Page 9: Detail of the "Yellow line" omnibus at the corner of Clay and Kearny streets, 1850s. Collection of Paul C. Trimble. Ad from *San Francisco Evening Bulletin*, July 23, 1863.

Page 10: Detail of a Valencia Street horse car at Market and Post streets, 1870s. Collection of Paul C. Trimble.

Page 11: Clockwise from upper left: Henry Casebolt's "balloon" horse car, 1871; City Railroad car at Montgomery and Market streets; Omnibus Railroad car beside South Park development on 3rd Street, 1879. (All colorized by the author.) All collection of Paul C. Trimble.

Page 13: Steam line car on Market Street at Third Street. Photograph by Lawrence & Housewworth. Cable cars at the intersection of Geary, Kearny and Market streets. Photograph by A.P. Flaglor. (Both colorized by the author.) Both collection of Paul C. Trimble.

Page 14: Market Street at 3rd Street, February 14, 1917. Collection of Jack Tillmany. 1896 *San Francisco Examiner* ad, collection of Emiliano Echeverria.

Page 15: Horsecar on Market Street. Collection of Paul C. Trimble.

Page 19: Upper image: *San Francisco Examiner*, September 22, 1895. Lower image: *The Strand*, November 1899.

Page 20: Upper image: *San Francisco Examiner*, April 11, 1895. Lower image: *San Francisco Examiner*, September 22, 1895.

Page 21: Collection of Angus Macfarlane.

Page 23: *San Francisco Examiner*, September 22, 1895.

Page 26: Author's collection.

Page 27: Detail from *San Francisco Bulletin*, July 11, 1896.

Page 29: "Interior of the Cabin," from *The Wave*, September 11, 1897. California Historical Society, FN-36643.

Page 30: Collection of Paul C. Trimble.

Page 31: Author's collection. (Colorized by the author.)

Page 33: Collection of Paul Melzer. (Colorized by the author.)

Page 35: *Four Track News*, January 1906. (Colorized by the author.)

Page 36: "A Vista Looking South," from *The Wave*, September 11, 1897. California Historical Society, FN-36642.

Page 37: *Country Life in America*, March 1907. (Colorized by the author.)

Page 39: Richmond District car house (Colorized by the author.) Courtesy of The Society of California Pioneers, San Francisco, C034491, C038656. Interior image by Charles Weidner, *Country Life in America*, March 1907.

Page 41: Collection of Emiliano Echeverria. (Colorized by the author.)

Page 43: "Car Town on the Beach, S.F., 1901," (Willard E. Worden photograph. Colorized by the author.) Courtesy of The Bancroft Library, University of California, Berkeley.

Page 44: "Cartown." (Colorized by the author.) Library of Congress.

Page 45: Vista del Mar. (Colorized by the author.) California History Section, California State Library, Sacramento, CA.

Page 46: Photograph by Fernando Cortez Ruggles. Collection of Jaci Pappas.

Page 47: Two left photos, collection of John Freeman. Two upper right photographs collection of Jaci Pappas. Color photo taken by author.

Pages 48-49: Construction and "Mr. McCullom's," (Colorized by the author.) California History Section, California State Library, Sacramento, CA.

Page 50: Vista del Mar. Courtesy of a private collector.

Page 51: Postcard of Vista del Mar. (Colorized by the author.) Collection of Glen Koch.

Pages 52-53: Details of photo on page 6. (Colorized by the author.) California History Section, California State Library, Sacramento, CA. Kitchen image from *Country Life in America*, March 1907.

Page 54: "Cartown." (Colorized by the author.) Library of Congress.

Page 55: "S.F. Carville, CA." California Historical Society, FN-23635.

Page 56: (Colorized by the author.) Collection of Emiliano Echeverria.

Page 58: Clipping of Mary Gunn. Collection of Natalie Jahraus Cowan.

Page 59: *Overland Monthly*, November 1908.

Page 60: *San Francisco Call*, January 5, 1902.

Page 61: *My Muse*, Xavier Martinez. Collection of Art Penniman. Car houses, 1300 block of 47th Avenue. (Colorized by the author.) Courtesy of a private collector.

Page 63: "Carville at Ocean Beach," (Colorized by the author.) San Francisco History Center, San Francisco Public Library.

Page 64: Coppa's postcard. Author's collection.

Page 65: *San Francisco Examiner*, October 3, 1897.

Page 66: Arnold Genthe photograph, *Pacific Monthly*, January 1907.

Page 67: Collection of Art Penniman.

Page 68: *Pacific Monthly*, January 1907.

Page 69: *The Lark*, Book I, No. 1. (Colorized by the author.)

Page 70: "Dr. Leek's two cars," (Colorized by the author, wheelbarrow image added.) California History Section, California State Library, Sacramento, CA.

Page 72: *Four Track News*, January 1906.

Page 73: Postcard from author's collection. Great Highway/La Playa detail, circa 1905. Courtesy of a private collector.

Page 74: *Pacific Monthly*, January 1907.

Page 75: Martinez self-portrait, *Pacific Monthly*, January 1907.

Page 79: *Four Track News*, January 1906.

Page 81: "Carville at Ocean Beach," (Colorized by the author.) San Francisco History Center, San Francisco Public Library.

Page 82: Glass slide of sand sculpture on Ocean Beach, (Colorized by the author.) Collection of Gary Stark.

Page 83: "Beach scene at Carville," Turrill & Miller photograph. Courtesy of The Society of California Pioneers, San Francisco, C034490.

Page 84: "Traver's Fort Car #2," (Colorized by the author.) California History Section, California State Library, Sacramento, CA.

Page 85: Dunes near Ocean Beach, Willard E. Worden photograph? (Colorized by the author.) Courtesy of a private collector.

Page 86: *The Graphic*, January 18, 1902. "Boatmen" car house, *Scientific American*, June 29, 1901.

Page 87: Great Highway/La Playa, looking south between Lincoln Way and Irving Street. Photograph by Fernando Cortez Ruggles. (Colorized by the author.) Collection of Jaci Pappas.

Page 89: Alexander Russell family photos. San Francisco History Center, San Francisco Public Library.

Pages 92-93: "Cartown, 1901." Courtesy of a private collector.

Page 94: Great Highway between Irving and Judah streets. Randolph Brandt Collection. Courtesy of Emiliano Echeverria.

Page 97: Detail of aerial on page 116. Courtesy of a private collector.

Pages 98-99: Left image: Roy D. Graves Pictorial Collection. (Colorized by the author.) Courtesy of The Bancroft Library, University of California, Berkeley. Right image & opposite: Photograph by Fernando Cortez Ruggles. Collection of Jaci Pappas.

Page 101: Upper image: 48th Avenue, south of Kirkham Street. Photograph by Harry O. Wood. (Colorized by the author.) Courtesy of The Bancroft Library, University of California, Berkeley. Lower image: Collection of John Freeman.

Page 102: Photograph by George Lengeman. (Colorized by the author.) Author's collection.

Page 104: Upper image: Gertie Mehrlens at her 47th Avenue cottage. Collection of John Freeman. Lower image: Author's collection. (Both colorized by the author.)

Page 106-107: Left image: Collection of Helen Sjoberg. Right image & opposite: Collection of Paul C. Trimble.

Page 109: Cora Older scrapbooks. California Historical Society.

Page 110: *Overland Monthly*, November 1908.

Page 112: Clockwise from upper right: Collection of Mark Adams; "Somerset Road House," California History Section, California State Library, Sacramento, CA; Collection of Mark Adams.

Page 113: Upper image: Albert Neate on left. Collection of Yvonne Cangelosi Wilson. Lower image: Courtesy of a private collector.

Page 114: Detail of south line of Quintara Street near 30th Avenue, November 22, 1943. (Colorized by the author.) San Francisco Department of Public Works.

Page 115: *San Francisco Chronicle*, September 1941.

Pages 116-117: Courtesy of a private collector.

Page 118: Author's collection.

Page 119: "Carville at Ocean Beach." (Colorized by the author.) San Francisco History Center, San Francisco Public Library.

Page 121: Jesse B. Cook Collection. (Colorized by the author.) Courtesy of The Bancroft Library, University of California, Berkeley.

Page 122: "Interior of a residence at Carville near Ocean Beach," San Francisco History Center, San Francisco Public Library.

Page 123: Malucelli photograph by author. Car house photograph courtesy of Ken Malucelli.

Page 124: Photograph by David Gallagher.

Page 125: "Anna Marie Adams in her home at 'Carville' near Ocean Beach," April 8, 1947, (Colorized by the author.) San Francisco History Center, San Francisco Public Library. Photograph of Frank Lemus by David Gallagher.

Page 126: Collection of Paul C. Trimble.

Pages 127-129: Richard Schlaich Collection.

Page 131: Photograph by Greg Gaar. (Colorized by the author.)

Page 132: Photograph by David Gallagher. Illustration by Doug Stern.

Page 133: Photographs by the author.

Page 135: Photographs by David Gallagher.

Page 143: Left: *Scientific American*, June 29, 1901. Upper right: Collection of Gary Stark. Classified ad from *The Ocean Breeze*, April 17, 1925. Car house sketch: *San Francisco Examiner*, September 22, 1895.

Page 144: City Railroad Car in Carville. Richard Schlaich Collection.

"Cartown," San Francisco.

Beach Distraction Day, 1913

OUT AT THE BEACH

Remember, when you are in need of a cook, or someone to do general cleaning work in the home, your need will be met in the person of Mrs. Julia Thompson, colored, living in one of the car houses at 48th Ave. and Judah St.

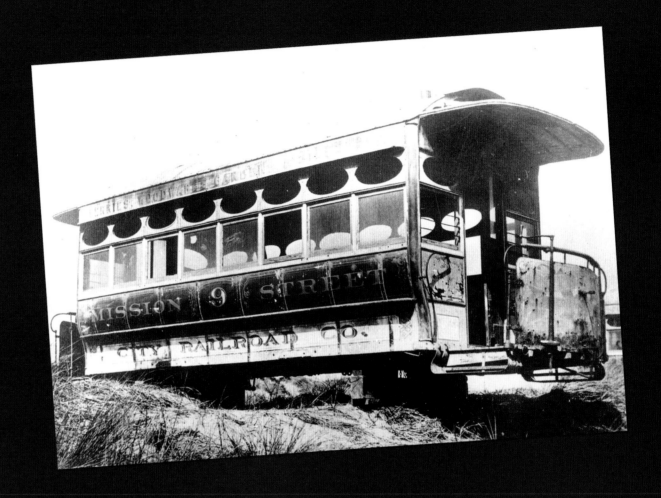